TO ALICE, NILES, AND ROMANE

PARIS STREET STYLE

A GUIDE TO EFFORTLESS CHIC

BY ISABELLE THOMAS & FRÉDÉRIQUE VEYSSET

UNDER THE DIRECTION OF CAROLINE LEVESQUE

ILLUSTRATIONS BY CLÉMENT DEZÈLUS
PHOTOGRAPHS BY FRÉDÉRIQUE VEYSSET

ABRAMS IMAGE
NEW YORK

Contents

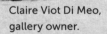

Claire Viot Di Meo,
gallery owner.

WHAT IS FRENCH STYLE?

The Cultivation of Effortless Chic

They envy us for the je ne sais quoi that is so characteristic of French style, the effortless, unstudied chic of it: the tangled hair of Vanessa Paradis, the faded jeans of Charlotte Gainsbourg, the masculine shirts and ballet flats of Inès de la Fressange, the look of Clémence Poésy.... French women are more sober in their clothes choices than the flamboyant Italians or the eccentric English. We live in a country where female elegance is anything but ostentatious.

The French fashion icons, recognized for their style the world over, have a thoroughly bourgeois appeal: Chiara Mastroianni, Audrey Tautou, Valérie Lemercier, Françoise Hardy, Isabel Marant—the least you can say of them is that not one is notable for extravagance. A long way, indeed, from Katy Perry, Courtney Love, or Donatella Versace. Even if they've spent hours getting ready, it doesn't show. The French woman is not overdone in any way. The French

> *American women are pulled together perfectly from the moment they wake up in the morning: perfect hair, varnished nails, high heels, the lot ... as if they were bound for a cocktail party or some other red carpet affair. French women don't bother their heads so much.*

Emmanuelle Seigner ACTRESS, SINGER

woman fears nothing; she will go out without fixing her hair, with unpainted nails, and no makeup. Despite her apparent dishevelment, she remains elegant. The wild side of her, which was the glory of Brigitte Bardot, has never gone out of fashion: often copied, never equaled. The French woman is also more accepting of the ravages of time and the consequences of occasional gastronomic indulgence—she loves a good gratin washed down with a bottle of Burgundy. Quite simply, the French woman is practical with good sense in matters of both food and personal style; her watchword is moderation—in all things, especially the best things. But the good news is that the French approach to style can be learned, and we are here to teach you everything you need to know!

 Foreigners say French women are gray and beige. They forget the details, and the nuances within the details. The allure of French women lies in simplicity, shown through a well-chosen handbag or a perfect pair of shoes. Americans tend to follow trends. Italians are more sophisticated. To me, Kate Moss in the Saint Laurent ad epitomizes Parisian elegance, with her slightly askew chignon; she's a chic woman, completely unstudied. That's my way of working; I like hair that shifts and moves. It doesn't have to be perfect to convey emotion.

Sylvain Le Hen HAIRDRESSER, FOUNDER OF HAIR DESIGNACCESS

Vouelle founder
Michelle Boor.

Inter view

MAXIME SIMOENS
designer

How would you define French style?

It's the de-structured elegance of an unostentatious female goddess. It's showing the body to its best advantage in the subtlest way, through the prism of a chic, timeless image. Mélanie Laurent, France's current girl next door, represents this well: Her elegance is untamed, but never excessive. Coco Chanel was the same, a woman who was liberated from all the codes, nonchalant, and elegant.

Do you think that the "French touch" still exists, in spite of the modern tendency for styles to become uniform?

Noble fabrics, embroidery, precious materials—which never descend into frippery—can never die, and because of that Paris will never be dethroned by any other fashion capital. Similarly, the savoir faire and quality of couture can never be matched by fast fashion. And elegance is also knowing how to live, a way of reacting, moving, and behaving. . . . I associate it with the places we live in, with our imagination, and with the daily objects that surround us. Women especially have the gift of feeling and understanding these broader aspects of elegance.

Is it out-of-date to follow the fashion?

"Fashion"! I hate the word. As far as I'm concerned, to follow the fashion is to be already out-of-fashion. Why should we adapt ourselves to the current era when we have the choice of being avant-garde or retro-vintage instead? All these rigid rules about lengths, shapes, and cuts are very 1960s. Today, luckily, the melting pot offers us more opportunities to be different. It's a matter of generosity and temperament. I prefer to think that dress is a means of creating an identity for oneself. Dress allows us to open up to other people and transmit our image. People who are covered in

monograms from head to foot project nothing but the depth of their pockets. People who set out to project nonchalance construct a disheveled look. People who want to send a more aggressive message choose more aggressive clothes. It's all pure sociology! Clothes can also be a defense. Throughout our lives we can continue to alter and develop our image.

What do you think is the most essential item for a woman's wardrobe?

They talk about the little black dress. It's quite true that black never goes out of fashion— you can wear it winter and summer. Chanel and Dior jackets or Balenciaga pants are high on many people's lists, but personally I don't care much for iconic stuff. Everyone must find their own best thing: It can be anything from a pair of jeans in which one has lived moments of powerful magic, to a jacket that shows off one's figure fantastically, or a simple dress that brings good luck.

Are there any clothes you would dismiss out of hand?

As far as I'm concerned, nothing is beyond the pale. Even sarouel [harem] pants and leggings are acceptable. I would only forbid phony rule making. If you succeed in reinterpreting an item of dress and find a way to wear it to good advantage, then everything is possible. It is, as usual, a question of style and chic; you can look great in 1970s Yves Saint-Laurent dungarees, or look like nothing at all. Same goes whatever your age. At sixty, you may not want to wear a miniskirt any longer, but if you're proud of your figure, there's nothing to stop you. If you think your knees aren't pretty or your arms are too slack-skinned, keep them hidden. Every woman has her complexes, her characteristics, and her special desires. I am for freedom of expression and for me that goes hand in hand with the freedom to dress as I please. The only limit to this may be found where self-expression ends… and vulgarity begins.

FIND YOUR OWN STYLE

THE ART OF WARDROBE MANAGEMENT

Not so long ago, people followed codes established by society and convention. Workers dressed as workers, bourgeois women as bourgeois women, schoolboys as schoolboys, widows as widows. At forty, you cut your hair short and forsook bright colors, you stopped wearing fishnet stockings if you were respectable, and you stopped wearing jeans to the office. Nowadays, most of the conventions and prohibitions in the matter of clothing have fallen away. So much the better. Except that, without this rigid but reassuring framework, some women appear to have lost the art of managing their wardrobes. Today, you join a tribe rather than a class and you stick to its fashion conventions or you don't: you have the choice. You can also find a style of your own according to your personality, your taste, your way of life, and your circumstances.

So, is style still important? Yes, because we express our idea of who we are by the clothes we wear. It's an unconscious, unspoken language that we direct at other people. A non-look makes us invisible; forced eccentricity frightens others, or amuses them. It's no coincidence that our choice of clothes for a first date makes us deeply nervous. If you're feeling uncomfortable in a bad outfit, you can wreck the whole business. Hence the importance of not disguising oneself, or of not wanting to resemble some friend, actress, singer, or business woman one happens to admire. You have to find your own look. There's no need to knock yourself out to stand out; all that's required is to be aware of who you are. If you are that, you can develop a harmony between your clothes and your personality. The exercise isn't necessarily easy—some women hit on a style of their own at an early age, some never do. But the good news is you can learn it. It's not a question of age or money, more of a state of mind and an intention.

Inès-Olympe Mercadal, the
founder of Mercadal Vintage,
updates her vintage imitation-
leather jacket and dress (found at
a flea market) with a designer belt
and Atelier Mercadal pumps.

Tidy Your Room

We all have a tendency to grab the clothes on top of the pile. It's easy, it's quick, it's usually risk-free, and we can dress pretty much automatically. What a shame, though, for the treasures that lay dormant for years, which you so confidently purchased, convinced that they were indispensable. So it's a good idea from time to time—say twice a year—to sort through those forsaken clothes. The process can be trying, but it's invariably worthwhile. First of all, forget the "two year rule," which has it that we should throw out anything we haven't put on for a couple of seasons. It's an archaic idea that has little sense if you want to preserve a complete wardrobe.

Throw Away!

• **Clothes that no longer fit you:** Out with the tight T-shirts you wore when you were twelve (you need them looser now), things that are the wrong length, straight pants cut too short, jackets with cuffs that are too broad (like from the 1990s), jeans that are cut too low on the hips or that are altogether too tight or too loose.

• **Worn-out, threadbare clothes:** Unless they have a nice patina, such as beautiful leather, they make you look scruffy. Throw away all coats and jackets that are frayed at the collar, at the elbows, or at the point where your bag rubs against them; balled-up pullovers; white shirts that have yellowed; tights with holes; down-at-heel shoes; and leather that has aged poorly.

• **Cheap, soulless clothes and accessories:** Toss bottom-of-the-line dresses that aren't cute anymore; badly cut coats, bought on the fly during cold snaps; a slutty dress worn once for a failed date; an old-fashioned suit worn on job interviews at the turn of the century; smelly leather jackets bought secondhand; the Hermès-style scarf that isn't Hermès; tired-looking fake leather belts; nineties pointy shoes; ugly ethnic jewelry made in China, bought at a duty-free shop on the way home from a trip abroad.

Keep!

• **Good-quality basic things:** Hold on to 100 percent linen or cotton T-shirts, cashmere pullovers that haven't balled up, white blouses, boots, perfectly shaped shoes, ballet flats . . . in short, your lifelong friends.

• **Pieces by known or lesser-known designers:** Don't even think about throwing away a Jean Paul Gaultier dress, an Ann Demeulemeester short jacket, a Vivienne Westwood jacket, a blouse by Alexis Mabille, a Comme des Garçons pullover, Weston boots, extravagant sandals by Pierre Hardy, an Alaïa belt, a scarf by Épice, and so on. Even if you wear them only occasionally, you will always feel a certain pleasure when you put them on. Items like these seldom go out of fashion and can always be combined with other basics, as well as with the newcomers in your wardrobe.

Organize!

• **Organize by season and by family:** You'll be able to see everything more clearly if you do, and you'll be able to spot new combinations more quickly. Instead of always pairing the same pieces, try being your own fashion editor, finding fresh shapes and outlines. That way you can pull together as many looks as possible from your repertoire of jackets, skirts, dresses, blouses, and shoes. Dare to blend genres, colors, and forms— try them on, try them out. You'll soon discover all manner of undreamt-of riches in your wardrobe. Take photos of yourself in the outfits you feel really good wearing.

Heimstone founder
Alix Petit's signature look:
biker boots and a feather
headband.

Assert Your Style

Read the magazines and blogs that match your sensibility; observe the styles in movies and on TV, noting what you find attractive. The goal is not so much to carbon-copy some movie star as it is to train and enrich your eye.

Spend time looking at yourself as objectively and neutrally as possible. Not in the mirror, whose reflection you know by heart anyway, but by focusing on your weak points, or else overlooking them altogether. For instance, you can study yourself in a favorite snapshot that corresponds to your idea of who you are. Be tender and indulgent toward yourself. Have you noticed your wasp-waist recently? Your fine bone structure? Your graceful neck? It's a good way to break away from any prejudices you might have about your body. How about a dress with a pronounced waist, instead of the shapeless smocks you may have worn for the last fifteen years? How about daring to wear a long dress instead of thinking it will age you? And you might stop believing for a moment that flat heels make you look shorter. The lesson is, before you dismiss a given shape or color, *try it*.

•••••••••

Some women—and some men, too—have dared to be different: Audrey Hepburn, for example, wasn't afraid to accentuate her androgynous figure and go against the conventional ideal of beauty of her time, which fetishized big bosoms and big bottoms. She embraced her own personal style. Hepburn is said to have been solely responsible for driving big bosoms out of fashion. As for Brigitte Bardot, she popularized ballet flats and gingham. Like those two, personalities such as Jackie Kennedy, Kate Moss, Sofia Coppola, Chloë Sevigny, and Dita Von Teese have all given their names to a certain style. Certain designers, too, have created their own unmistakable signatures: Jean Paul Gaultier's sailor jersey, Karl Lagerfeld's high collar, Paloma Picasso's lipstick, Sonia Rykiel's flamboyant mane of hair, the feather headband of Heimstone's Alix Petit. Everyone should find a signature of their own if they want to stand out from the crowd.

Annina Roescheisen's most extraordinary accessories are her tattoos. She got her first tattoo at the age of thirteen.

A pre-Raphaelite beauty, she emphasizes her femininity with formfitting dresses and vertiginous heels.

Joëlle Dufag, a sales associate, never leaves home without dozens of ethnic-chic bracelets on her wrists.

But don't change yourself radically. Don't adopt a style you can't see yourself wearing just because the sales girl said you looked sexy in it. You have to learn how to feel "right" in your new clothes, and how to please yourself. Working on your appearance can turn your life upside down. People will look at you differently, and your own attitude toward yourself will change—especially if you're in the habit of hiding in black, or in shapes that mask your figure. If you're afraid of too radical and sudden a change, proceed by slower degrees: Taking a classic base as your starting point, add color and fantasy by using accessories (scarf, shoes, bag). You'll soon get a taste for this exercise and want to take it further.

Take time to go shopping and visit an array of different stores. If you're the shy type, bring a friend along—not necessarily the most fashion-conscious one you have, but one whose taste in matters of fashion you appreciate. Once again, you don't want to follow the trend of the moment; what you need is to find the style that suits you best. Try to break out of your established set of colors and shapes. The only thing you risk is being pleasantly surprised. Try them all: pinup girl, hippie chic, business woman, English lord.... The aim is not to disguise yourself but to prove to your own satisfaction that you can dare to do what you want. De-dramatize the whole business. Enjoy yourself.

A clothes shop is the best psychiatrist's office. I take the time to help women try things on, but I also listen to their anxieties. My clients open up their lives to me; they entrust their bodies and their uncertainties to me. And it often happens that a piece of clothing helps to resolve those uncertainties.

Sandrine Valter CREATOR OF THE AESCHNE BRAND

Alexandra Senes
mixes souvenirs
from her travels with
designer pieces (Céline,
Margiela...).

Interview

ALEXANDRA SENES
trendsetter

How do you see fashion in this day and age?

A brand like The Kooples is representative of what is happening today. It was born out of nowhere in five minutes by the simple expedient of lifting information from magazines and riding the current codes of fashion: young, old, music labels.... This is a trap into which we should never fall. Today, to modernize a brand, they pick out the same old art directors, along with the rocker of the moment, and the most fashionable writer... mind-blowing. And then the things of the moment—the fake spectacles, the blue hair, the Balenciaga fringed handbag. These are not for me. Is there any room left for curiosity? Ordinary people no longer know how to appropriate trends and these things are fashion disasters.

Do you think the French woman will be able to remain independent of all this in the future?

Yes, because she has a definite style of her own, she doesn't go around trying to buy one. She succeeds in making brands stylish just as English women do (but in a different way). She will customize a Kelly bag, or wear a Charvet shirt with a fluorescent skirt.... Unlike her Spanish, Italian, or Swiss sisters, she knows how to play with her wardrobe. She can give a twist to the way she dresses that is entirely her own. Whether it is classic, Bobo, or goth, she can construct something around it. Plus, she has a deliciously unkempt side to her: She can get away with out-of-control hair, untrimmed fingernails, a minimum of makeup. I remember an American woman who had just met Vanessa Paradis asking me, "How did a dirty girl like that get to be a star?" In France, thanks to fashion, even fat women know how to be beautiful. They're educated, and they can judge proportions and volumes to perfection.

Who would you nominate as your own quintessential French woman?

She'd be a blend of the ultra-elegant Edmonde Charles-Roux on account of her intelligence, Inès de la Fressange for her laugh lines, Anna Mouglalis for the voice, Camille for the scruffiness, and Emmanuelle Seigner for the insolence. Farida, Azzedine Alaïa's favorite, is a symbol of the elegance of tomorrow: She represents the mixing of genres and elegance in every sense of those terms, and especially in the attention she pays to others. The great muses are genuinely elegant, and the It Girls just aren't. The genuine articles are the kind of women who, like Olympia Le-Tan, inspire creators and delight magazine editors.

What is the role of fashion in your life?

I founded a magazine, *Jalouse*, which was always six months ahead of the trends, and I've been following every fashion week for many years. So I know fashion inside out. But if we're talking about my personal wardrobe, I prefer to manufacture my own style. The bag or the outfit that everybody wants, well, they're something I don't even see; they hold no attraction for me. When I'm dressing, I begin with the shoes and after that I improvise according to how I'm feeling. I never wear jeans. I dress in colors to set myself apart from the fashion girls. I spend my time playing around with combinations of classic and loud clothes, things that aren't symmetrical, wonky things, missing sleeves, three stripes going off in different directions, colors that don't go together, high heels with socks, summer clothes in winter, fantasy tights.... I love things that clash, and I hereby formally claim these errors of taste as *my style*. People often tell me, "You're the only person in the world who could wear that," or "You're the original African blonde!" It's true that I left Senegal, where I was born, at eight years old, and went to live in New York. So I guess the clash is still taking place inside me.

What clothes do you carry with you everywhere you go?

A man's shirt, made by Céline or by Dior (preferably the Dior one with a reversed collar); my leather jacket (My Way by [Aurelia] Stouls), which I can wear just as easily with a bathing suit as with evening clothes; my Codognato wolf skull ring that is a hundred years old; and an old Margiela sleeveless fox-fur coat that is just as comfortable in hip company as it is with people who couldn't give a damn for fashion. I'm lucky enough to be able to buy quality items exclusively. If I don't go to H&M, it's because I just can't find the right colors there: They never seem to have the red or the yellow I'm looking for. A good Marc Jacobs yellow will always remain good. I have only one small regret, and that is I don't have the eye to buy vintage clothes. But I do have friends who can find exactly what I need in secondhand shops.

SHOULD WE KEEP UP WITH FASHION?

OR SHOULD IT KEEP UP WITH US?

There are two schools: women for whom the words *slim-fit*, *flare*, *7/8*, *platforms*, *derbys*, *head-bands*, *treggings*, *pencil skirts*, *stilettos*, *carrot pants*, etc., belong to a foreign language, and women who speak that language fluently. The former don't care about fashion, or at least *think* they don't care, because:

- "It's not my thing; I don't have the figure for it."
- "It's expensive."
- "It's superficial."
- "I don't understand it."

The latter have mastered the codes involved—more or less. They use them to create their own personal fashions, or to copy whatever the latest trend imposes, and sometimes without giving the matter much thought and in spite of what really suits them.

Between these two attitudes there is a fine balance, which many women find difficult to strike. In general, French women are pretty good at locating this balance. They know how to blend new things into their wardrobes to create their own personal style, and they have the instinctive chic to get *themselves* noticed before people notice their clothes. This is simply because their clothes *are* them. They like following the fashion trends, but nevertheless they have understood that it's not taboo to mix things that are straight off the catwalk with earlier collections that are still contemporary or even timeless. They are more inclined to respect their own personalities than to apply a trend.

(Bad) Excuses:

"It's not my thing; I don't have the figure for it."

Given the abundance of styles available, despite that fashion designers prefer "shrimps" to girls of more generous dimensions, any woman in the world can find a shoe and a dress that fits her—and that includes really unusually proportioned women who have serious trouble finding the clothes they want. Sometimes we have to spend a lot of time in order to find good things, and sometimes we have to rely heavily and craftily on accessories.

Learn to see yourself with new eyes, and know how to make the best of your good points. Legs and breasts aren't everything. Look at the nape of your neck, at your throat, your waist, your curves, and your bone structure; emphasize them if they're good, rather than dwelling on their imperfections.

Ideally, you should accept yourself as a complete article—that's exactly what the people who love you do. Who said broad shoulders ruled out wearing a sleeveless dress or that calves on the thick side were incompatible with skirts? In short, be straight with yourself, but open to new possibilities. Today, the choice of clothes is so vast that any woman can dress exactly as her personality dictates, and be stylish without necessarily following the prevailing fashion. All the better. There's no such thing today as *the* fashion, but many fashions. The magazines may try to boss us around, but we're much freer than women were twenty years ago. Have you noticed how radiant women are when they're manifestly comfortable with themselves and with the clothes they wear?

> ❝ *I hate the idea of copying the latest trends. One's allure doesn't necessarily depend on what one's wearing. In my book, a person with style is someone who has grace and a kind of bloom about them, who knows themselves inside out, who knows what suits them and plays with it.* ❞

Pascale Monvoisin JEWELRY DESIGNER

"It's expensive."

Nowadays, this excuse has no credence whatsoever. You can dress yourself quite beautifully for 100 euros by shuffling beautiful basics with bargains, such as a little piece from a major fashion house or a hip chain store and a few cleverly selected accessories. It isn't necessarily such a great idea to amass four trendy jackets at 35 euros each; sometimes it's better to dip into serious capital to procure a piece that will last for many years. It isn't because you're rich that you know how to dress. You need curiosity and daring in the mix. Elegance may be an innate quality that has nothing at all to do with money, but the fact is, we can *learn* to dress stylishly and we can *learn* to avoid making certain mistakes.

"It's superficial."

Is that so? Do you think the image of yourself that you project to others is a superficial thing? If so, it's a shame, because the people you meet are bound to take your measure according to the way you look. "The house you live in is just as much the property of people who look at it, as it is yours." The old Chinese proverb still holds true.

"I don't understand it."

No problem—we're here to explain it.

A Question: Should We Yield to the Temptation of "It"?

Today, we tend to remember the defining aspects of the time, such as Vanessa Bruno's sequined tote, Balmain's torn T-shirt, Zadig and Voltaire's cashmere, Isabel Marant's platform sneakers, Charlotte de Darel's handbag . . . all "It" things. So do you go along with them? Certainly not, if you're just trying to reassure yourself and be part of the It Girl club. But why not, if the object of everyone else's current desire happens also to correspond with what you want and who you are? The only risk is seeing lots of other women wearing the same items at a given moment. Singularity is probably preferable. In a time when luxury is a mass industry, the surest and greatest luxury is the one-off.

Michele Boor opts for timeless pieces: a black dress (p. 25) and wide-leg trousers by Aeschne worn with Vouelle sequined ballet flats.

66 I'm sure that many women suffer terribly from not being blond, blue-eyed, and buxom. There are plenty of silly guys who have this cliché in their heads and make no secret of it! So the women get complexes about not being the stereotype and resort to camouflage. Women have difficulty working out what will please their men, and above all what suits them personally. They buy the same dress as a friend who is built the same way, without stopping to think if it really suits them. Ninety percent of my clients are drawn to pieces that don't begin to match their style. The plump ones make a beeline for the little-girl dresses with shoulder straps, and the women of forty see themselves as Lolitas. 99

Valentine Gauthier DESIGNER

66 I don't believe in trends. For me, elegance is being in sync with oneself. I find myself more attuned to Charlotte Gainsbourg in jeans and sneakers, than to Charlotte Gainsbourg wearing Balenciaga. I'm nothing to speak of in my jeans and T-shirts but if I'm going out to meet someone who interests me, I put on a pair of my good shoes to raise the level a notch. Shoes actually change the way my figure looks. 99

Annabel Winship SHOE DESIGNER

66 *Yes, one can take possession of one's body with clothes. We tend to dress up the bits of ourselves we like best, and neglect the rest. Try doing the opposite: concentrate your efforts on the parts you don't care for and dress them prettily. Appreciate everything your body has to offer. Take pleasure in it, don't invigilate it. Never forget that sensuality comes from within.* 99

Patricia Delahaie SOCIOLOGIST

66 *For me, style is all about having your own identity and not being a slave to fashion. It's about having class and a certain look, be it classic or otherwise. It's someone you notice in the street because she has her own personality and does not follow the latest fashion trends. I design for women who have a style of their own. Women who like my jewelry are truly independent. Perhaps they work in fashion, or in another creative field. Their age is of no importance, I am only interested in their personality: cosmopolitan, open-minded, enigmatic, and adventurous.* 99

Adeline Cacheux JEWELRY DESIGNER

Isabelle Thomas in a Roméo Pires tunic.

Catherine Lupis-Thomas, owner of the 1962 shop, shortened and embroidered her Replay jeans and wears them with an old Prada shirt.

Marie Hugo, fashion writer for *Glamour*, mixes brand names (Topshop boots, Kookaï sweater, The Kooples jacket) and designer names (Burberry skirt, Gucci belt, Fendi clutch).

A Swildens suit worn with men's shoes by Zadig & Voltaire.

Fashion has become a business, more than a profession that people love working in. We are fed too much information about it and the same products are exhibited and publicized everywhere. There's a surfeit of marketing that plays on a pseudo top-of-the-line, luxury image, which is false, and by which the consumer is manipulated. I show you a luxury ad, to justify the high price of my pullover—but in the end, the quality of my pullover is wretched. I believe we need to return to a correct and real system of consumption. We need to get back to a sense of real values, whose disappearance has killed industries and crafts and obliterated whole areas of skill—especially in France. The proliferation of young, creative talent today augurs very well. Between the stars who monopolize our billboards, and the magazines that chatter about trends, how can we nurture styles of our own these days? I suspect that for many women out there, shopping is a painful business. It's terrible to watch them tearing their hair out, but at the same time, allure is a major ingredient in our relationships with others. Clothes have always occupied an important place in our lives, and that's nothing new.

Amélie Pichard SHOE DESIGNER

All of these opinions were published in the blog *Mode Personnel(le)*.

Interview

CHRISTOPHE LEMAIRE
**artistic director of Hermès women's
ready-to-wear department, founder and stylist
of the Christophe Lemaire brand name**

**How would you define
French style?**

The search for balance and
harmony has been a constant
feature of French culture
throughout history—and we're
still searching. British culture
today tends to be baroque,
excessive, and fantastic: That's
not our way. Nor do we have
the refinement of dress that
is so characteristic of Italians.
No: French style is wittier and
more intellectual.

**Do you think French
women succeed in
escaping the uniformity
of modern trends?**

With the onset of mass
culture, women are certainly
not dressing as well as they
did before. Nevertheless,
H&M and Zara have made it
possible for people of limited
means to tap into fashion,
sometimes with great success.
That said, we all have to make
do with what is on offer and
what we can afford. French
women retain a strong
sense of sobriety and a good
understanding of detail. Even
if this is gradually being lost,
they still know how to make
themselves desirable without
overdoing it, and they still
have a subtlety and humor
that is uniquely French.

**Would you say that
clothes help us to express
ourselves?**

I would go further: Clothes
are the surest vehicle of self-
expression available to us. To
dress oneself is not futile—
it is an act of profound
significance. I believe in a
style that expresses the inner
self, that is neither a shell
nor a disguise for it. To wear
clothes is to be oneself, to
dream oneself, to be aware of
who one is. Dressing allows
us to sublimate ourselves
and to have fun doing so.

I am disgusted when I see articles, or films like *Sex and the City,* that relegate women to the status of idiots, thrilled by the latest handbag or the prospect of bargain sales in the shops. Even if there is a grain of truth here, it's worse than a step in the wrong direction. We should understand women's vulnerability, not laugh at it, and help them to feel seductive and secure.

How can we find the style that suits us?

First of all, know who you are. This is an introspective exercise and it involves brutal honesty vis-à-vis yourself. If you're looking for a disguise, you're running away from the truth. It's a path you have to take. It has nothing to do with money or information from the outside. You have to look at yourself, understand your body, work out which aspects of it need to be emphasized, find what goes best with your skin tone and the color of your hair. Who would you want to be? What do you wish to express? Even though appearances can be deceptive, we judge other people more or less consciously by their clothes, their way of moving, and their way of speaking.

What are the basic quality items that a woman should spend substantial money on?

There's no hard-and-fast rule that applies to everybody. Everything depends on the person you are. You have to find your own personal uniform—and "personal" is the key word here. You have to find your own vocabulary.

I believe very strongly in quality. Jean-Louis Dumas, the president of Hermès, used to say that when you buy a beautiful and expensive object, you forget the price but you remember the quality. I would say yes to a beautiful pair of boots, or top-quality pumps … provided they suit you perfectly.

Would you make an exception in the case of the little black dress that suits everyone?

For one thing, not all women like wearing dresses! There's nothing obligatory about dresses, and anyway, I strongly mistrust any form of diktat. People should dress as they see fit and according to their personalities. In civilized countries nowadays you're perfectly entitled to be eccentric if that's what you want to do. I think that's wonderful! We're even ready

to tolerate a man who wants to dress as a woman, so the very notion of good and bad taste is highly disputable.

Has the meaning of the word "sexy" changed in recent years?

Women wish to be desirable. Men also wish to be desirable. That is perfectly normal. But the word "sexy" is so overused and reductive now that I personally don't like to use it anymore. The notion of sexiness has become sad, impoverished, and synonymous with "cheap." I compare it to what pornography is to eroticism. It's like having breast implants and showing them to the world. "Sexy" today is the aesthetic of expensive prostitutes. I am very sensitive to feminine charms, but I prefer things to be hinted at—by a lovely nape, delicate features, perfect skin, magnificent hair, or a certain way of moving. So corsets and skintight clothes are not necessarily pleasing to me. I believe you can be sensual as well as modest. Modesty is in itself desirable. And I believe the vast majority of men—and women—agree with me.

FALSE ABSOLUTES

CLICHÉS THAT ARE HARD TO DISLODGE

Leopard skin is vulgar. Black makes you look slimmer. Slim-fit is for skinny people. Clogs are ugly. Velvet makes you look like a school mistress. Navy blue is what your mother wore. Flats are for tall girls. Nobody wears miniskirts after thirty-five. All of these clichés immobilize and intimidate us when we're casting about for a style of our own.

Fashion is something intimate and personal. Even if every single one of us wanted to be unique, we would still be drawn to buy what everyone else is wearing. It's reassuring. The brands, many of which do more marketing than fashion proper, are aware of this and take advantage of it. No, fashion has little to do with wearing the same thing as all the other women in the world. We *can* develop our own style, even if to do so we have to go against the trends and the clichés.

The über-chic fashion
editor Agnès Poulle.

High Heels Are Sexy

Yes, on condition that they're well chosen (nothing is worse than cheap high heels), fit right, and you know how to walk in them. Yuck! The little toes clamped around the edge of the sole, the foot bulging out of the shoe leather, and the gait like a stork in a minefield. Not all high heels are chic, anything but. What makes a shoe sexy is the line of it and the way it makes us move, certainly not the height of the heel. The proof of this is that you can be very feminine wearing ballet flats.

Push-Up Bras Are Irresistible

Naturally, a rounded bust is delicious (oh, the breasts of Scarlett Johansson!). But many men—and many women—agree that the sweet trembling bosom of Vanessa Paradis is equally devastating. So why do so many women insist on wearing nothing but push-up bras? Of course, you have every right to accentuate your bosom. You also have to select the kind of underwear that best suits your size: Nothing could be worse than embroidered lace bras showing through a sleeveless T-shirt or a tight sweater. And beware of showing little rolls of fat under your arms.

Leopard Skin Is Vulgar

Yes, if the material is cheap and well-worn. If you scatter it around a more sober outfit, there's no risk. Our favorite leopard skin items are V-neck cashmere pullovers, chic fake fur coats, trench coats, woolen or silk scarves, smart loafers and pumps, and clutch bags.

Anne-Sophie Berbille, co-founder of Prestigium.com.

A leopard-print dress
by Roberto Cavalli and
Jimmy Choo sandals.

Student Nastasia Frydman wears plaid pants by Gunhild.

Sequins and Spangles Make You Look Like a Christmas Tree

It's best to wear them in the daytime. Like animal prints, they simmer down when mixed with more conservative clothes. A sequined cardigan will spice up a pair of jeans, sequined derby shoes will bring a breath of fresh air to a pair of pants or a classic dress, and a scarf will galvanize a sober coat.

Checked Patterns Make You Look Like a Lumberjack

They may also make you look like a a bumpkin or a cowboy.... Checks have to put up with all manner of prejudices, yet in their essence they're easy to wear, flattering, and never really go out of style. According to the outfits or accessories with which you coordinate it, this chameleon pattern can be punk or English aristocrat. Your Scottish trews will look totally different if you wear them with classic loafers or Doc Martens. Checks can also affect other aspects of dress: A checked cowboy shirt will add a touch of modernity to an office-type pants suit and spice up a dinner jacket or a sweatshirt. Another bonus is that checks can blend easily with other patterns: checks and a liberty-type print, checks and polka dots, big checks and small checks.

Vouelle ballet flats.

Carrot Pants Are for Slim Girls Only

Not at all. The cut hugs the hips and hides the buttocks without flattening it. Choose pants cut high in the waist, made from a fabric of substance, and wear them high and tight to the body. After that, what you do is a question of taste—but maybe it's not your thing, or your man's.

Ballet Flats Are Always Chic

Depends. They can quickly turn old lady–ish. Avoid the plastic ones (it's awful when you take them off), thick rubber soles, too high-cut or angled heels. The only ones worth a damn are superthin-soled and open almost to the toes. These look as good with jeans—straight or slim fit—as with short and knee-length dresses.

Short Socks Are for Little Girls

True enough. Socks with sandals or socks with moccasins don't work for everyone. You need to be pretty sophisticated to carry them off. But pretty, paper-thin Lurex socks with heels, or brightly colored funky ones, can delightfully and stylishly feminize men's shoes.

Fat Girls Shouldn't Wear White

There are no particular colors that are the sole preserve of thin girls, blond girls, pale girls, dark-haired girls, or redheads. That would be much too easy. It's all a question of style, material, and cut. Naturally, when one has generous curves, it may be best to steer clear of soft, white linen pants or leggings (actually everyone should forget about the latter). A really ample woman can look fabulous in a tuxedo or a white sheath dress, provided the fabric isn't elasticized or low-waisted.

· · · · · · · · · ·

Ouch, My Poor Feet!

To break in shoes that are a trifle narrow or just too new, wear them around the house, with socks on, ten to fifteen minutes a day. If you're still in pain after that, take them to a cobbler, who can stretch them half a size larger. Once that's done, immediately put them on to finish the job.

Playful pairing of Miu Miu
socks and Vouelle sandals.

Black Suits Everybody

"Take the black one, it goes with everything!" says the salesgirl when she's fed up with waiting for you to make up your mind. But what she says isn't necessarily true. Contrary to what people think, a black handbag or black shoes won't go with any more items in your wardrobe than fine Bordeaux red ones, deep scarlet ones, or chic anthracite gray ones in a beautiful material. And black shoes definitely don't look good with bare, white legs. You need to select your materials with great care. Nothing looks worse than a suit or a pair of pants in non-crease polyester, an unfortunate uniform that legions of women wear to the office these days.

Velvet Is Jean-Pierre Léaud

The actor Léaud and the signature disheveled look of many of his characters may have been an inspiration for punk's alternative style, but while velvet can be punk and scruffy if you like, this is only when it's dirty and loose. When velvet is well-cut and fits you, it can look great. Nothing beats a jacket of smooth velvet or stiffish corduroy to give structure to your shape. In the best spirit of Britpop, one might dare to wear a velvet suit with a flowered shirt and a lavallière bow tie. As for stretch corduroy pants, they're perhaps more casual but are otherwise a worthy substitute for jeans. Try them in soft colors: rust, pine, khaki, caramel, chestnut, plum, Indian pink. The sheen of real velvet is more delicate. Also, a good option remains the body-hugging evening dress. In any event, shun velvet if it looks limp or threadbare, or if its color has faded.

· · · · · · · · ·

Ouch, My Poor Wallet!

An expensive piece from a famous fashion house carries no guarantee of quality. Today, many designers have their clothes mass-produced abroad from fabrics bought by the mile and finished shoddily. In the last twenty years, the quality has dipped as sharply as the prices have risen. They take us for fools.

Leather Makes You Look Like a Musician

No comment on the ponytail-earring-and-paunch-leather look. Since the invention of stretch leather, the old ghastly material that bunched around your buttocks and knees is a thing of the past. If your figure allows, try a leather sheath or pencil skirt. Otherwise, look for pants, or a knee-length flared skirt, which is perfect for hiding ampler aspects of oneself that are better concealed. Avoid the all-leather look unless you're an Elvis doppelgänger. If you're planning to wear pants or a skirt made of leather, leave your bomber jacket and sandals in the closet and temper any remaining ambiguity with a fabric that can soften its rough edge: a semi-transparent silk shirt, for example, or a tweed jacket. Bear in mind the erotic potential of leather, as demonstrated in the photographs of Helmut Newton. And look seriously into the question of color: Black is far from the only one; there's also blood red, plum, caramel, and navy blue.

Not exactly a roadie: Romane Gréze, a student, wears a leather jacket over a flowered dress.

Romane in Maje
leather leggings.

Fashion writer Claire Dhelens adds a touch of glamour to a Céline suit with a Léonard shirt.

Inter*view*

SANDRINE VALTER
**creator of the
Aeschne brand**

What, in your view, constitutes a beautiful fabric?
At first, it's the tactile sensation it gives you. When you touch a piece of clothing, the fabric should be soft. Next, read the label: It will describe the fabric's composition. Always opt for natural materials like cotton, silk, and wool, not forgetting viscose, which comes from tree bark. But look out—there are many, many different textures of cotton, silk, and wool. Some cottons are low-grade whilst others have the same feel—and the same price—as silk. It's a question of weave and treatment. Hence the importance of the way it feels. To verify whether or not a woolen coat is top-quality, do as I do when I buy my fabrics: Rub two pieces of the material together. If it balls up, that's a bad sign. You can do the same test on cashmere.

Should we rule out synthetic materials altogether?

If synthetic materials form the bulk of a fabric's composition, as is the case with very low-priced brands that make everything shiny, it's plain ugly. But we shouldn't condemn synthetic things out of hand. They have their virtues. For example, light can "burn" silk. After ten years, they say that 100 percent silk clothes are "cooked," whereas a minimum of synthetic ingredients can strengthen them and make them last longer. A little polyester and acrylic will prevent a pullover from balling up and make it washable in the machine. Anything that is pure wool, including cashmere, will eventually ball up. Elastane makes fabrics more elastic and comfortable. The ideal proportion of synthetic material in a piece of clothing should not exceed 5 percent. You'll find it written on the label.

How can we recognize beautiful, high-quality finishing?

Turn the garment inside out. If it's as beautiful on the inside as it is on the outside, that's already a very good sign. I use silk—never polyester—to line my coats and jackets. It's more fragile but it's also more beautiful. Quality is crucial but quality also needs to be well maintained. It's a matter of choice. Check the places where pieces of fabric are sewn together: For example, checks or stripes should be perfectly aligned. And check the threads and whipstitches: Is there anything hanging off? Are the hems round, or do they hang limply? Are the buttonholes neat and well defined? Are the buttons themselves solidly attached? If you see any stray threads around the buttons, that's a sign that they've been put in by a machine, because the machine has yet to be invented that can do a holding stitch (or *point d'arrêt*). Because of this, machine-mounted buttons will always fall off sooner rather than later. Buttons in general should be carefully examined: Plastic is stronger than mother-of-pearl or glass but not nearly as chic. When clothes are mass-produced, the work is done in a hurry and the finish is invariably botched. It's a pity, because an outfit can be genuinely chic only when details like these are perfectly executed.

What would you say is the definition of a beautiful cut?

A piece of clothing that falls right when you're wearing it and in which you feel perfectly at ease. Don't rely on the way it looks when you see it on a coat hanger. Even if the designer is excellent, if he or she is working with a technical designer or pattern maker who is merely average, the product won't be much good. Just like a house designed by a bad architect is bound to collapse, so a dress can go off the rails if the technical designer's work is botched. For example, if he or she draws on a computer, as most mass-production designers do nowadays, the fall of the dress will be nonexistent. A good technical designer should take full account of the female figure and work in three dimensions on a real model. If you've suddenly discovered that the clothes made by a brand you like no longer fall properly, it's always because the technical designer has changed. Hence the importance of trying clothes on yourself before you buy them. And of being curious about clothes that catch your eye but are not necessarily that good-looking when seen on a hanger: Seen on you, they might be fabulous.

AS IN FASHION, SO IN LIFE

FRIENDS YOU CAN COUNT ON

Our best friends are the clothes that stay with us, that are always there in times of severe distress. Fashions may shift and change, our bodies may evolve and develop, our courage may waver, but we can always count on these articles of clothing. Even if we have neglected them for months and years, or they've been pushed to the back of the closet because we didn't think them fun enough or because they always told us the same story, one day we'll come back to them with renewed delight. Best of all, they don't mind. And their absence has made them even more attractive and desirable.

Clothes like these are the basics that always go with the fashion of the moment, and which the patina of time makes ever more beautiful. The one condition of their loyalty is that we have the sense to pay dearly for them at the start. In other words, we must pay all due attention to the quality of their fabric, leather, and finish. It cannot be repeated often enough: If anything is worth investing real money in, without skimping, it is clothes of this kind.

The following are the true friends we hold dearest. Maybe you have some of your own you would like to add to our list, or since you can never have too many friends, perhaps you may wish to make a few new ones.

A Burberry coat worn punk-style.

Trench Coat

After Lauren Bacall popularized the tight-belted trench coat, Jane Birkin and Charlotte Gainsbourg gave it contemporary chic by wearing it casually with sneakers and jeans. The trench coat is now much more than just something you wear in the rain; it has become a definable, recognizable outline. Still, it has to be cut in high-quality, substantial gabardine. Along with the leather jacket, it is one of the few items of clothing that looks better well-worn. It's no coincidence that old, trustworthy Burberrys can invariably be found at flea markets and in secondhand clothing stores.

Boots

For generations, the boot was exclusively worn by men (in fact, the wearing of boots was one of the capital charges brought against Joan of Arc at her trial). It was Courrèges who brought boots out of men's wardrobes and made them available to women in general. Since his time, from Hermès to Louboutin by way of Isabel Marant, designers have tirelessly reproduced their own version of the boot, both for winter and summer.

Boots are essential at any age and well suited for a variety of occasions. We buy motorcycle boots in our later years of adolescence, in token of rebellion. In our forties, we wear them to add spice to an outfit that otherwise would look too conservative. We like to wear *camarguaise* boots (the

•••••••••

Choose Your Trench Coat with Loving Care

Give priority to the material, not the name. Avoid synthetic materials and droopy cotton with a shiny or scuffed finish. Look for a true gabardine, wool that's rough to the touch, or leather like in The Matrix. *Never overlook the quality of the lining, which gives body to the coat, or the details (epaulettes, leather buckles on the cuffs, front pockets with flaps).*

Ann Demeulemeester boots.

Actress Priscilla
de Laforcade in
classic Burberry.

Nastasia wears a Gunhild lace top, H&M jeans, and Ash boots.

Marie Jacquier, director of communications for the National Museums in France, in Balenciaga pants and Ann Demeulemeester boots.

French equivalent of cowboy boots) and riding boots in natural leather with shorts and summer clothes, and we bring them out again to wear leisurely with jeans or a pair of straight or flared velvet pants. We soften them with polishes and creams, we resole them and we buff them constantly, because we like them to shine like the boots of an English lord. *Camarguaise* boots are coming back with a vengeance, so we can take them out of the closet now or buy a new pair. They can be worn with skirts and colored tights or, more conventionally, with jeans. The riding boot looks just as good with Jackie Kennedy WASP-style clothes as it does with a miniskirt or denim shorts.

Tropéziennes

Oh how a thin leather sole with a few straps on a tanned and beautifully pedicured foot can be the summit of elegance. You have the choice between a 40-euro pair that will auto-destruct in three months, or the real McCoy, made by a skilled craftsman. If you want your *tropéziennes* to last for more than one summer, buy them from Rondini, either in Saint-Tropez or on the Internet. Yes, they'll be more expensive, but that's the way it goes if you want quality.

White Shirts ... Or Black

Girl's blouses, invariably too tight and slim cut at the waist, are no longer on the menu. Instead, go to your man's closet and make off with his most beautiful shirt. No terylene—only straightforward, thick, beautiful cotton, preferably without front pockets and shoulder straps. It will look supersexy as a dress, belted tight and worn with nothing else. It will add something extra to the simplest pair of jeans, and lend class to the shortest shorts. It will modernize a straight skirt or a severe pencil skirt. In short, it will do just about everything. Our favorites are Dior Homme, Charvet, Agnès B., and Gap.

V-Neck Cashmere Sweaters

You need one of these—you can wear it fitted, or loose so it slips craftily off the shoulder. This suits any woman, whatever her build, and can avert many a sartorial catastrophe. It looks good worn with a pencil skirt, enlivened by jewelry, or with a sober jacket with a buttoned collar and pants. During the week or the weekend, depending on accessories, the cashmere sweater projects sophistication or casualness, just as you like. In common with the white shirt, it can be shrewdly accessorized to glide—without missing a beat—from a business meeting straight to a tête-à-tête dinner. You don't even need to spend a lot of money on it—the ones sold at Monoprix in Paris are perfect. If the fabric balls up, buy yourself one of the electric sweater shavers that can be found in most hardware stores to remove the fur balls. They'll disappear like magic. *Always* hand-wash your cashmere in tepid water (any other temperature is fatal), using special wool soap or—even better—a mild shampoo. Tumble dry as gently as possible until just slightly damp and finish the drying by laying the sweater out flat on a towel.

> *My single most important article of clothing, the one I always have with me, is a black pullover. I've got masses of them; they're the basis for a look on which I can graft other, stronger elements.*

Maria Luisa

FASHION EDITOR OF THE PRINTEMPS
DEPARTMENT STORE (*ELLE*, JUNE 24, 2010)

Chinos

Chinos are the brothers of jeans. These unisex American pants made of cotton duck, with or without pleats, can be worn broad, narrow, long, short, or rolled up at the cuffs. Stylish French women avoid wearing them with sneakers and sweatshirts. Much too casual! They prefer to marry their chinos with men's shirts or Scottish plaid shirts, or a fine silk blouse and jewelry, a vest and a man's jacket, chic sandals with heels, or boots. We like them in every color and cut—and we specially like them brand-new.

Pea Coats

Corto Maltese wears one at all times. Saint Laurent made it a classic and he was a perfectionist. However, the pea coat looks really elegant only if it's made of thick woolen fabric, slightly coarse to the touch—just like the original.

Shop manager Julie Bocquenet wears an H&M top, Zara chinos, and an Hermès scarf.

Short Leather Jackets

Fashion has explored and reexplored the potential of the short leather jacket for many years, with mixed results. Choose it in supple leather, soft and cut close to the body, then let it acquire a patina as you wear it as your armor and second skin. Don't be afraid to wear it with your skimpiest, most romantic dresses; they'll go very well with it. Our favorites are from Swildens, Gerard Darel, Virginie Castaway, Heimstone, and Rick Owens.

Yes, you can find it.

• • • • • • • • •

The Proper Care of Leather

Baby cream and cleansing cream are very good for cleaning and maintaining fine leather clothes. Put a little on a cotton pad and spread it in circles all over the surface without rubbing. If the color starts coming off on the cotton pad, stop immediately and take your jacket, coat, skirt, or whatever straight to a dry cleaner who specializes in leather. And if you want to put it away for a while, turn it inside out, wrap it in tissue paper, and store it in a sealed plastic bag.

• • • • • • • • •

How to Maintain Your Best Clothes

1. Never store them uncleaned; they'll be eaten by moths.

2. If possible, vacuum pack them with peppercorns, which are the best non-allergic, non-polluting moth repellent.

3. Prevent shoe leather from cracking by regularly applying moisturizing cream, and by keeping them in shoe boxes or stuffed with newspaper.

Interview

ALAIN CHAMFORT
singer/composer

Who would you say best represents the quintessential French woman today?

Thirty years ago, Catherine Deneuve embodied the kind of perfection that satisfied the codes of the moment; Inès de la Fressange is probably the last active symbol of that perfection. Today, you could say Kate Moss is the one: a little beat-up, a little rock 'n' roll! And if the truth be told, elegance itself has become something of a myth, since mass consumption is what really dictates the trends. On the other hand, a perfect individual image calculated to the last detail is scarcely more interesting than what mass consumption throws up. There has to be a certain casualness about dress....

You're saying that the very notion of elegance has evolved?

I can't really tell any more. For me, elegance is the result of a certain dress, a certain attraction, and a certain refinement. It's the result of a bourgeois education ... which doesn't necessarily guarantee any result at all. In the old days, people were capable of spotting beautiful materials and beautifully cut clothes.... Now they have less interest and indeed less of an eye for things like that.

Do elegant girls still exist?

Yes! I would say that an elegant girl is one who is lucky enough to be able to wear anything she likes without looking contrived. She has common sense, she knows how to wear the right outfit for any given situation, and there's always a certain underlying humor about the way she dresses. Above all, she knows how to spotlight her own personality without appearing to resemble anyone else. We should never forget to remain ourselves—I think that's vital. And we should never forget how our clothes reveal what we have in our heads. Our choices in that department emphasize who we are.

What's the worst thing you can think of, in terms of bad taste?

My number one hate is Capri pants! They create an appalling line.... Number two is the thong, even in the strictest privacy. I hate to see asses exposed! Even if the girl is really stunning, it's just plain vulgar. I've no objection to seeing the outline of panties showing through a pair of pants—I'd rather see them than a G-string. And finally, don't ever imagine that a clingy miniskirt and high heels can be remotely sexy! Everything about you that is seductive can be ruined by a dubious choice like that.

Romane's authentic
Schott Perfecto jacket,
in bubble-gum pink.

THE POWER OF ACCESSORIES

DETAILS THAT ADD AN EXTRA OOMPH

Not all of us have the means to buy a new coat every winter, or to buy the clothes of the moment. With the explosion of major brand names and the phenomenal success of some of them, we are much more likely these days to find ourselves wearing the same things as our neighbors; we take less and less risk, everyone copies everyone else, and in the end everybody looks alike.

But with a selection of cleverly combined and understood accessories, one can animate, modernize, and give breadth to one's wardrobe, especially since today's creators of accessories are overflowing with ideas that can make us look unique. Accessories can alter the *humor* of the way you look. They can make your look more your own.

Actress and Canal+ feature
editor Aude Pépin accentuates
her APC overall shorts with a
vintage belt by Alaïa.

Michelle does not hesitate to wear shocking pink tights with a yellow dress by APC.

Tights

Tights are mostly bought just because you need to be warm or because you don't want to go around with your legs uncovered. But you are wrong to take them for granted. Chosen badly, they cheapen everything (flesh-colored ones are a case in point). Handled correctly, they can wake up an otherwise drab ensemble and revitalize your appearance. Tights, in fact, are a relatively cheap accessory that can revolutionize the way you look. Forget about sheer tights combined with a short skirt or a black dress, unless you seriously want to look like a provincial lawyer's elderly assistant. If you're afraid of making an error of taste, go for black opaque; but colors aren't the sole preserve of little girls. Abandon red (which can be dangerous when associated with black); opt instead for violet, anthracite gray, luminous fuchsia, lilac … all are superb with khaki and fall colors in general. You can combine them with chic ethnic dresses, short skirts, velvet, or denim. Beware, though, of looking like a rainbow, by layering on too many different colors. Stick to a few complementary shades.

Lace and fishnet tights go just as well with classic straight skirts as they do with a little cotton dress or leather shorts. They can be worn with pumps, boots, or sneakers. If you're feeling brave, you may like to try tights with socks and sandals.

But tights printed with flowers, butterflies, and the like should be treated with extreme caution. You don't want to look like an old hippie.

Scarves

We prefer the big, out-and-out *chèche* scarf to Scottish plaid or lumpy beige ones that immediately make you look like a grubby student just out of class. What exactly is a *chèche*? It's a broad piece of colored fabric, ethnic and exotic.... "It's what the Tuaregs wrap round their heads," explains Yaya, an expert on the subject and the creator of Yaya Store in Paris. "You could call it the only makeup in the world that needs no remover." In winter, a scarf lends warmth and light to our overcoats, just as it does for our friends the men. It works well coupled with a classic outfit, or with such basic elements as trench coats, men's jackets, or leather jackets. In summer, if it is broad and thin enough, as in the case of scarves often termed as sarongs or pareos, you can wear it as a wraparound skirt or a dress, leaving a bare back. Bring them back from trips abroad (Borneo batiks, fine materials from Africa, Mexico, or Asia). Or else, if a flight to an exotic destination is beyond your means, check online for scarves from the Yaya Store, Épice, or Antik Batik in Paris.

Playful combination of fishnet tights and Louboutin pumps.

• • • • • • • • • •

If you have a good stock of scarves, make the most of them: Try tying one tightish around the neck in combination with funky clothes, around the head sixties-style, gypsy-like with big hoop earrings, or around your waist.

Yaya Store owner Yaya wearing her famous neck scarf.

Atelier
Mercadal
sandals:
jewelry for
feet.

Jeweled Sandals

Because they can give jet-set allure to the roughest pair of jeans or the dullest khakis, you should maybe splurge once in your life on a good pair of jeweled shoes. But beware: (1) Don't flaunt your wealth: Wearing them in a low-profile way is always the best; (2) Make sure the feet you're displaying are absolutely perfect, properly pedicured, varnished, and polished. Nothing is worse than cracked heels and ugly, ill-kept toenails. You can wear these shoes in the winter with Lurex socks. Some of the best, most beautiful shoes like these come from Atelier Mercadal, Manolo Blahnik, Antik Batik, and Vouelle.

The Single Precious Piece

A big item of some kind will instantly set off the most ordinary dress, add a touch of femininity to a professional pants suit, or lend sophistication to jeans. For best effect, do without your other perennial jewelry (ten-year anniversary emerald ring, fantasy baubles, fat watch). Your big piece should have no competition.

A selection of "good" ones: a plastron necklace with colored glass balls and a grosgrain ribbon (Marni); a mass of long gilt chains (Imai); a heavy silver chain (Adeline Cacheux); a big cuff (Aimé).

High-heel sandals by Charles Kammer.

· · · · · · · · · ·

For Feet As Soft As a Baby's

At night, after delicately washing and buffing your feet with fine soap, blend a little Avibon cream with Neutrogena cream for dry feet. Apply generously, then wrap both feet in Saran Wrap, pull on some cotton socks, and go directly to bed. If you're sleeping with someone, just keep the wraps on long enough to watch a couple of episodes of Mad Men.

Alice Hubert's "La fumeuse" necklace is always a hit, especially when paired with a Claya jacket with a leather collar.

Louboutin—shine on!

Headbands

Not seen since Woodstock, but now coming back, are vintage pearls, delicate peacock plumes, plaited metal mesh, extravagant flowers, crazy feathers, and delicate chains to adorn the hair—and not just the hair of teenagers. The headband has reemerged as a key accessory for women who like to have fun with fashion.

··········

Scrunchies and Worse

Shun imitation-horn hair grips made of plastic, or fluorescent velvet items. These are things that should never be seen outside the bathroom. The same goes for Hello Kitty mini-grips and the colored knickknacks shaped like dragonflies that look so sweet on little girls. Anything that implies that you just got out of bed or the shower should not be worn. Kate Moss or Inès de la Fressange wouldn't be seen dead wearing anything of the sort. There is simply no excuse for them: There is no shortage of pretty hair accessories available from all the major brands and designers (Sylvain Le Hen, Johanna Braitbart, Libertie Is My Religion, Pascale Monvoisin).

Law student Naphsica Papanicolaou wears an American Apparel T-shirt and a hair accessory by Hair DesignAccess.

Something borrowed: journalist Marie Peyronnel wears her mother's mythic Agnès B. leather jacket from the 1980s.

Belts

You're stingy about belts? Don't be. A cheap belt made of something awful, a surface gilded but aging, a crusty piece of leather, an ounce of cheap metal can make anything look vulgar. Hence it is imperative to avoid wearing belts of fake leather. Even pants made by a top brand won't save them. As with shoes, there can be no half measures with belts: Cheap leather is very, very seldom chic. It's better to opt for fabric instead, namely the thick canvas belt that is still a feature of army uniforms. A belt not only holds your pants up, it also completes the shape you are looking for. A simple, high-quality leather belt raises the tempo of a bargain-price jacket, a masculine belt can modernize a trench coat, and a straight-cut dress will be made superbly feminine by a broad belt of tight elastic.

Hats

Between the Queen of England's Sunday hat and Boy George's something else, there is a middle ground. It's always said that some people have heads for hats, others not, but since there are so many different types and shapes of hats, there really is one to suit any head. A man's hat is zero risk; you can be any age—from fifteen to ninety—and it will go with anything you feel like wearing, from a lacy romantic dress to a tweed jacket. Ditto, a colored "summer in Capri" sun hat.

Press agent Patricia
Chelin wears a man's cap
from H&M and a ring by
Sandrine de Montard.

Interview

ALIX PETIT
**creator of the brand
Heimstone**

**What do you think of
fashion today?**

I think we're totally
submerged by the mass
market. I'm not against
people making money, but I
think these days consumers
are being treated like idiots.
Clothes are expensive, but
most of them are being made
in China and are of terrible
quality. What makes them so
expensive is the marketing
that seethes around them;
quality and the savoir faire
aren't part of the equation.
Clothes are no longer made
to last. They're supposed to
be consumed and replaced
immediately.

My aim is to make clothes
that last years and are good
for any time of year. I don't
understand why at the end
of each season a piece of
clothing loses 50 percent of
its value. I like things that are
timeless and never go out
of fashion. Who cares about
the seasons? Why from one
season to the next shouldn't
a particular piece of clothing
still have the right to exist?
Why can't I wear my summer
dress in winter, with woolly
tights and a warm pullover?

For my collections, I
spend as much time
designing models as I do
designing my fabrics and my
prints; I control everything
from A to Z. I do that to add
value to them, to give them
individuality. I don't want
to come across designs like
mine anywhere else. I want
my work to last and I want it
never to go out of style. You
can like my designs or you
can hate them, but I think
you'll agree they're unique.

What are your influences?

I have no fashion influences
to speak of and I care little
for trends. I don't read
women's magazines much.
I very seldom go to fashion
shows, because I don't like
the way they do fashion. As
far as I'm concerned, clothes
shouldn't make women into
stereotypes; they should
represent us, express what we
really are. Traveling influences
me, as do ballets, books,
music, encounters with
other people; in fact, just
about everything influences
me except what I see in the
fashion world.

I design the kinds of
things I personally like
wearing, and I don't care if
they're not all the rage. If
I want to use yellow, I use
yellow, whether it's the
"in" color or not. I have no
barriers inside my head, I
can mix and blend prints
and colors as I please, I have
no problem doing that. I
set out to build something
unique in the shop that has
human dimensions. I dislike
big department stores in
general: The idea that I'd go
to buy clothes, drink a glass
of wine, and have lunch all
in the same place gives me
the creeps.

How would you define your own personal taste in clothes?

I've never really had a particular style, and the way I dress is no more than the reflection of myself. I've always done that, ever since I was a teenager. And the women who come to my shop either have clearly defined looks of their own, or feel invisible and want to raise their profile dramatically with something original.

How do you rate French women, as they appear in the street?

I think French women in general are classical and beautiful. When I see them around New York they look more combative and liberated than they do here. Women come from all four corners of the world to New York, and I can tell you there's no shortage of spectacular French ladies in that cultural melting pot. In New York, a French woman will happily match an old pair of boots with a very short skirt and a good tattoo ... in Los Angeles, she'll look more glamorous, Hollywood style ... but everywhere I see her, she has an elegance that Americans can't match.

Do you think fashion is influenced by consumer society?

Yes, and it has been for years. We're led to believe that if we dress like such and such a man or woman, we will become in some way that person. We no longer dress because we *are* something but because we *want to be* something. Women have been convinced that they need to resemble such and such a celebrity, but *I'm like this, so I'll damn well dress like this* is the way they really should be thinking.

Our society is heavily influenced by TV culture with its phony realities. People want to be famous, without doing the work. They think they can call themselves artists just because they've taken a few photographs. Work is no longer recognized or acknowledged. I believe many people in my own generation have no idea what work even means.

And do you see the same facile tendency in the world of fashion?

The materials are much less beautiful than they were before. More and more synthetic rubbish is being bought, and more and more crap is being turned out by the mile in China. Beautiful pieces made by great designers and produced by top brands are constantly being copied by mass fashion organizations, and consumers have fallen into the habit of buying things cheap whose development and manufacture cost their original creators a fortune. Sometimes the manufacturers of these items are incapable of any finish at all; they're more interested in making a quick buck than in doing good work. Many actually skip certain stages in the manufacture of a piece of clothing—and make no mistake, this happens in France and Europe just as often as it does in India. I'm afraid that a whole limb of painstakingly acquired knowledge has withered away, and the culture of beauty no longer exists at the heart of certain textile industries. Profitability is everything, so any number of stages have been "simplified" at the expense of quality. It has become much, much more difficult and rare to find people prepared to work on the principle that each garment should be unique and of the highest quality.

MAKING CHEAP LOOK CLASSY

HOW TO WEAR
MASS-PRODUCED CLOTHES
WITH STYLE

Style has very little to do with money. Elegance and originality are qualities that can't be purchased. If they could be, we'd all go looking for inspiration from the richest people in the world. It's precisely a lack of means that makes certain people so creative.

Today, the trend is for blending and mixing clothes, and we should take full advantage of it. And we shouldn't forget that while mass consumption has made it possible for vastly more people to know about fashion trends and appropriate them, moderation will always remain the essence of good taste.

Ariane Dubois, founder of
the A de la Roche brand,
adds a vintage button to
her simple top.

Give In to the Urge But Use Discretion

If you don't want to look like everyone else on the subway, steer clear of everything you see in advertisements, in shop windows, and in stacks on prominent displays in the store. The search for authentic nuggets of real value requires plenty of time and a good eye. You have to get out and about often, even though the risk of falling for stuff that's in fashion is thereby increased. Tip: Call your local H&M store to find out when the wholesale deliveries are made. What a joy it is to unearth a black half-leather, half-cotton T-shirt, or a pearl-gray silk shirt that you may—wrongly—have thought uninteresting at first glance. As you search in stores like H&M, avoid cheap basics, and forget about V-neck sweaters in "cotton jersey." Likewise, black pants that are already too wrinkled, jackets with too many zips, too-shiny fake-satin tops, clingy jersey dresses made of synthetic materials, over-faded jeans with too many metal bits, over-faded Indian blouses, plastic belts that are just too plastic. Don't expect them ever to be good basic items that will last. With very few exceptions, what you'll find in bargain stores are things that are good for a season.

Fred Marzo shoe.

A neo-bourgeois look
for Ariane Dubois: H&M
skirt, Paule Ka jacket, and
Céline scarf.

The surprising combination of this Mimilamour necklace, leather shirt by Ann Demeulemeester, Antik Batik belt and skirt by Monica's Vintage, and Surface to Air sandals lights up the pavement!

Put Your Trust in Accessories

Every day we come across elegant, stylish Parisian women who amaze everyone by saying the little dress they're wearing came from H&M, Zara, or Mango. *Believe me, it's perfectly true!* The craftiest French women understand the need to juggle their accessories, because they're what make the difference: a pretty scarf, a fine belt, designer shoes. Yes, these things might cost the same as two or three pairs of pants from the aforementioned brands, but when you already have ten pairs of skinny jeans, you can probably do without an eleventh and invest in something beautiful that will last for years and enliven your look, such as a jeweled belt or shoes by young designers like Annabel Winship, Jancovek, or Amélie Pichard.

Mix

Never opt for a single, one-dimensional look. To have real style, you need to know how to put together designer + cheap + vintage clothes. This rule holds for all brands and all budgets. Mix a basic with an accessory that adds an original personality, presence, and allure.

Customize

Personalize your clothes. Even without a sewing machine and with very little skill, you can replace "industrial" buttons with ones you bought in a hardware store (or snipped off a piece of clothing you no longer wear); sew on a badge to add whimsy to a waistcoat or a jacket; add an embroidered collar to a pullover, or a scrap of fur to a jacket or an overcoat; cut off the top of a T-shirt leaving a raw edge; shorten a man's sweatshirt with scissors; or cut a long skirt of transparent lace back to mid-thigh.

Customize and bejewel your H&M parka.

Dauphine de Jerphanion in her customized parka and bag by MySuelly.

Leopard and lace, stylishly paired
by Agnès Poulle.

Cheap Shoes Are Unforgivable

Low-priced leather nearly always ages very poorly—and if there is one thing you shouldn't skimp on, it's shoes. When you go to a job interview, your prospective employer will instantly look at the state of your fingernails and the quality of your shoes. An unpolished shoe, scuffed and with the heel worn down on one side, and the faint outline of toes that bad leather betrays, will condemn you. A vulgar-looking pump can spoil the effect of the classiest dress, while a simple, refined sandal will make your jeans look ultra-chic. Though you may not be mad about shoes (is that possible?), they're accessories that you should cosset and renew at frequent intervals—unless you've invested in an array of classic shoes that patinate well and rise above transitory fashions. And please pass this message on to our friends the men!

The Wrong Glasses

Beware of invisible, transparent-type glasses that give you the impression you haven't been outside your apartment since the late 1990s. As for "original" frames (butterfly, double-sided, metallic), they won't survive certain associations. For example, you can't blend red plastic glasses with a chic dress—they'll make you look like an escaped circus diva. Beware, too, of opticians who are determined to lead you into bad habits. You're the one who's going to wear fuchsia-colored glasses on your nose all day, not the salesman who convinced you to buy them. Don't hesitate to take all the time you need, take photos of yourself, go back to the shop several times … and trust the kind of optician who refrains from putting the latest signature models in his window, preferring to rely on "real" glasses designers, tried and true. You'll make no mistake if you opt for a no-frills classic design with a simple, uncomplicated shape (Meima). Even in optical matters, train yourself to think vintage. Scour the flea markets—retro frames in tortoiseshell or imitation Bakelite are currently in favor. And certain shops still stock real classics like Meyrowitz's Manhattan.

Inès-Olympe Mercadal wears a red Zara dress, a belt she bought in India, and Atelier Mercadal Vintage shoes.

66 *I choose my clothes on the principle of the* coup de coeur. *I couldn't care less about labels. If I like it, I'll buy it. Cult items don't interest me. I never really caught the snobby bug for certain labels or pieces, and actually I waited twenty years before I got my first Burberry. I don't like the kind of trendy accessories that everyone seems to want, or rather that the industry tries to impose on us. I love altering my clothes, cutting them up, re-dyeing them, adding details, customizing them. Also I buy vintage outfits that I bring up-to-date. I carry them back from my trips abroad. In the U.S., the choice of these is unbelievable. A few months back I bought a cheerleader's jacket that I now wear with a knee-length straight dress; I adore it. In general, it seems to me that women today are short on audacity, in spite of the outlandish propositions that filter through to them from the fashion catwalks and the press. They don't dare step too far out of line and even the youngest ones are liable to be too conformist, even too uniform in their approach. They're heavily influenced by the glitzy people they see in the press,*

and by the red carpet look that has been uppermost for a few years now. I hope we in France don't end up with the kind of unfortunate situation Italy's in at the moment. The "bimbo" style that flooded Berlusconi's Italian TV has managed almost entirely to eradicate the kind of wonderful woman that Italian neorealist cinema revealed to us in the 1950s and 1960s.

Recently, I met an amazing lady in a tiny village in the Aubrac, who dresses exactly like those mythical actresses. She wears the pretty silk blouse, the Chanel-style tweed skirt, the high-heeled Louboutin-style shoes, and all that with a certain carelessness.... She's simple and superb, with a very contemporary, modern look that's all her own but coupled with a classic style.... She's far more daring, I'd say, than most women in the big cities.

One can project an illusion by one's way of dressing, but if one isn't elegant and generous in oneself and in one's behavior in society and vis-à-vis other people, well, one isn't really elegant. Elegance in this life goes hand in hand with the way one is and the way one handles oneself. 99

Agnès Poulle FASHION EDITOR

This lace skirt by Zara looks even sexier after the lining is shortened to show a little leg.

Tara Jarmon
top, Mango belt,
Bershka leggings,
Minelli pumps, and
Desigual clutch.

· · · · · · · · · ·

Spoiling the Effect

The washing-instructions label left on a scarf: *How many times, riding the subway, have you itched to get out your scissors and snip off the label on the woman sitting next to you?*

The sticker on the sole of a shoe: *Did you think nobody would notice?*

The transparent bra strap: *Just as the strap of a bra languidly showing on the shoulder off of which your cashmere sweater has slipped can be bewitching, so can a plastic bra strap make you look supercheap.*

Unflattering undergarments: *Beware the panties that have a quadri-buttock effect and the bra that makes folds in your back.*

Clothes that are too tight or too loose at the waist: *If they bunch up or stretch too taut, that's very bad.*

Balled-up fabric: *Don't try to frantically remedy this with your fingers. You can buy practical little machines (electric sweater shavers) that do the job fine, and thus breathe new life into a jaded pullover or coat.*

Misplaced hems: *The length of sleeves and hemlines of pants and skirts should always be perfect—especially beware pants that are too short or that drag on the ground.*

Interview

BERTRAND BURGALAT
singer/composer

© Photo Serge Leblon

What does being elegant mean today?

Elegance isn't based on money; it's based on charm and intelligence. Nothing can be nicer than to see people dressed in an interesting and singular way, provided it happens to suit them. It is not a question of means or education but of one's relationship to conformity. To be elegant is to find a nice way of counterbalancing the injustices that prevail in society. And also of fighting against the way people's bodies are being bullied into uniformity.

Would you say that fashion leads the way to style?

Fashion has never been as omnipresent as it is today. But again, money has nothing to do with elegance. You can't just buy a certain brand of clothes and be suddenly chic. So much the better! Nevertheless, this was exactly the reaction of millions of people, who thought they were hip because they were all wearing clothes with the same label, listening to the same music, and going to the same cliché hotels…. What's happening today in fashion is what the music world went through twenty years ago: a period of waste and greed driven by marketing. Today, they expect us to obey their commercial decrees of what is "in" and what is "out." To go along with this is to demonstrate the kind of feebleness and conformism that prove you have no taste whatsoever. I have a similar total lack of respect for people who buy superexpensive shoes for themselves, but pay their temporary workers next to nothing.

Do you think that to have a personality is to accept the risk and responsibility of making mistakes?

Yes, but I also have immense sympathy for people who make mistakes in the way they dress. I approve of individualism, provided it's not demonstrated by a complete getup of some kind. What I really can't stand are expensive ugly things like those 1980s heavy shoes that waitresses in Iron Curtain countries used to wear. When one buys oneself an expensive and luxurious item, out of respect for the people who sweat over such things, one should try to buy something that looks good. I prefer a pair of shoes that are plain wrong to luxury phony-intellectual ones. The wrong shoes are infinitely more touching.

Do you think women have become more chic in the years since fashion began to be democratic?

Well, I think they've become more feminine, but they wear their clothes in such a conformist way that half the charm is lost. Take the current fashion for ultra-high heels: it's so unsubtle, predictable, and stupidly generalized that one can't even begin to get interested.

CONDEMNED WITHOUT A FAIR TRIAL

THE GOOD, THE BAD, AND THE UGLY

From time to time, fashion manages to surprise us. It offers up improbable clothes that make you think, *Never, in a million years, would I be seen dead in that.* And then, after a few months of steady pressure from magazines and store windows, you find yourself wearing that improbable thing on your back or on your feet. Even so, even after our eyes have grown accustomed to them, pieces of this kind remain very difficult. You have to wear them with moderation.

We've put some of the most notorious, controversial items in fashion on trial here. And it turns out some have gotten a bad rap over the years. Worn with a bit of finesse, the following items can be wonderful parts of your wardrobe. However, they also come with a bit of risk. While there are exceptions to every rule, our general guidelines should help you avoid making a style faux pas.

Dauphine de Jerphanion wears a Givenchy T-shirt over Falke leggings and many necklaces by Marni and Alexandre Vauthier and a Marc Jacobs bag.

Capri Pants, Calf-Length

NEVER: The wide model, in limp linen, with pockets on the sides and/or sliding laces, combined with a fourteen-year-old's T-shirt, girly sneakers, or monk's sandals. Help!

YES: It's tolerable in the Audrey Hepburn style, close to the body and tapering; that is, more like 7/8 or toreador pants, sober and chic, worn with ballet flats, fine leather sandals, or pumps cut low across the foot.

Skinny Pants

NEVER: The low-waisted Lycra model that crushes the ass and reveals the crack and combines so horribly with a mini T-shirt or a jersey tank top riding above the belly button. Ugh.

YES: In jean, cotton, leather, or waxy stretch, perfectly form fitting: These you can wear from dawn to dusk. If you've invested in the right pair, you can even promote them to the level of basic indispensable. They will go just as well with a loose T-shirt as with a classic silk shirt, ballet flats, or biker boots.

Leggings

NEVER: Ass huggers, like in the eighties, worn as a substitute for pants.

YES: Donned in lieu of tights, between seasons, with a skirt or a dress. It must be acknowledged that they look better if you have slender calves and pretty ankles.

Bermuda Shorts

NEVER: The just-back-from-the-seaside version, with a pastel-colored turtleneck and yachting shoes.

YES: The "boyfriend's old denims" version, threadbare, in summer, with high sandals so as not to interfere with the line of the leg. Or in winter, cut longer, in the supermasculine style with a tweed jacket, woolen tights, and lace-up Oxfords or Chelsea boots. If your figure is voluptuous, you'll need to be taller than average to carry them off.

Vinyl leggings (Religion) add a rock-star touch to the Eva Zingoni tunic and Vanessa Bruno shoes.

Polder's colorful tights worn with Michel Vivien sandals brighten up Clarisse and Marine's otherwise classic look.

Zebra-patterned pants by H&M are perfectly paired with an Isabel Marant jacket, a Balenciaga T-Shirt, and a vintage fur that casually brushes the ground!

Animal Prints

NEVER: Acrylics or cheap materials. Leopard skin, snakeskin, a zebra pattern, and the like require a certain amount of finesse, and should never be paired with turquoise eye makeup, dark brown lip liner, or terra cotta blush.

YES: In discreet touches (on wool or silk scarves, Trilbys, ballet flats, furry boots, or handkerchiefs) or else as your main item (fur jacket, printed trench coat). Animal prints should be worn raffishly and freely, or not at all.

Down Jackets

NEVER: In town (makes you look like your brother-in-law, and the same goes for men).

YES: In the mountains or in the country. Go for the authentic down jacket or the sleeveless one; avoid anything smacking of fantasy and anything glossy or belted.

Cowboy Boots

NEVER: In the original version (jeans + biker jacket + cowboy swagger) or with a straight skirt.

YES: As worn by Marilyn Monroe in *The Misfits* (boyfriend's denims cut over the boot + white shirt) or offbeat (with a lace skirt).

> **❝** *I love cowboy boots. But never with jeans, makes you look too cowboy. I wear mine with my legs bare, with a flounced skirt bought at H&M, a jean jacket, or my beautiful Céline leather jacket.* **❞**

Emmanuelle Seigner
ACTRESS, SINGER

Long Skirts

NEVER: Just above the ankles, with pumps (you'll look like the patroness of a charity).

YES: In the ultra-long, romantic, Greek style, worn with laced shoes or *tropézienne* sandals and a man's jacket. Or else in Laura Ashley–type tiny flower prints with clogs or platform shoes. Contrary to popular belief, you don't need to be tall to wear a long skirt.

Never, Never, Never

UGG Boots, Moon Boots, Converse after your twenty-sixth year, quilted jackets, black tergal pants, jogging clothes in velour, cropped T-shirts, baseball caps, comic strip T-shirts, socks and underpants with motifs on them, long down coats, ties printed with something droll, velvet hair grips, plastic hair grips anywhere but in swimming pools.

Marie Courroy, founder of Mode Trotter, in a long skirt by Zara and a clutch by IRM Design.

66 *The things I most rule out are lip liner and false nails. And cheap, poor quality high-heeled shoes. Few things can be worse than that—but on reflection, maybe a stuffed bra under a T-shirt is.* 99

Yaya FOUNDER OF THE
YAYA STORE,
RUE MONTMARTRE, PARIS

Actress Constance Labbé pairs a long skirt by Opulence with an American Vintage T-shirt.

Wearing a charming and daring mix of prints, Julie Bocquenet looks stylish in an Isabel Marant top, vintage wool jacket, skinny pants by Zara, and wedge sandals from André.

Inter view

JEAN-CHRISTOPHE HÉRAULT
perfumer

Given that perfumes today are designed to please the world at large, would you say there is still a specific French style in the perfume industry?

Yes, thank God. French women tend to like *chypré* scents that leave a sensual, bewitching, hyper-feminine, refined trail in their wake— like Chanel's Coco, Clinique's Aromatics Elixir, or Mitsouko by Guerlain.... In general, French women prefer to use scent discreetly; it's a matter of respect for other women and the perfumes they may be wearing. In the United States, women like greedier types of perfume that are much more aggressive. In Germany, warm, strong, vanilla-based perfumes predominate, while in Japan you almost never smell perfume on a woman.

If you were asked to design a perfume to represent France, what would be your first reaction?

I think the image of Marion Cotillard would immediately spring to mind. For me, she epitomizes French beauty, radiating feminine charm with an aura that is both refined and natural. She is the antithesis of the sophistication favored by American women, who cannot go out of the house unless their hair is blow-dried and their hands fully manicured. The sophistication of French women is down to detail: the association of two colors, the choice of a single piece of jewelry.

Would you say that perfume reflects personality just as much as clothing does?

In the choice of a scent, you have much more freedom, fewer codes to obey, and no real age restrictions. A middle-aged woman will seldom go into a teenagers' clothes store, whereas she can quite easily wear the same perfume as a young girl. For example, a perfume like Angel is liked by different generations. In spite of everything, our olfactory preferences express our personalities and intentions. An extremely sensual woman may surprise you by opting for fresh and delicate floral fragrances over something more robust. This is another proof that appearances are not enough to determine the full complexity of another person.

Sometimes we can wear the wrong fragrance, just like we can wear the wrong clothes.

As a rule, that's a mistake that is short-lived. We have a carnal relationship with scent; if we don't feel good with it, we say it's "off." What we don't like is usually some kind of feeling it expresses. Even if the image, the bottle, or the brand play a part in our selection of a perfume, we should not content ourselves with sniffing it for only five minutes in the perfume shop. One should take the time to try it out fully on oneself, to spray it all over, and to live with it for a whole day before buying. It may be invisible, but the choice of a scent is no less important than the choice of an outfit.

DENIM FOR EVERY DAY

DRESSING FROM MONDAY THROUGH SUNDAY

The official uniform of American workers in the twentieth century, also adopted by Marlon Brando, the Hell's Angels, and Jane Birkin, continues to stalk the world's streets and fashion shows. We've come a long way since 1975, when Hélène Gordon-Lazareff, the founder of *Elle* magazine, forbade her fashion editors to come to work in jeans. Only after her death did jeans appear in the offices of the bible of French fashion. Though jeans are still banned in certain offices, they remain by far the world's top-selling item of clothing.

Jeans are like men; there are millions around, but very few that suit you. You can spend a lifetime looking for the one pair that will give you the ass of your dreams, and maybe never find it. Because contrary to what the magazines tell you, there is no such thing as a standard pair of jeans for all physiques. That would be way too easy. It's more a question of proportions and allure. The good news is that you can be amply proportioned and still look fine in jeans—even in skinny ones. Look at Marilyn Monroe in *River of No Return*, or Tara Lynn, the lovely size-48 model, who looks ultra sexy in a 7/8 skinny pair and retro pumps. The problem is that jeans are often worn wrong, as a last resort. In fact they constitute a state of mind, which can put up with anything but carelessness. They need you to take a minimum of interest in them. So you should pair them with something better than an old T-shirt—a check shirt, a tuxedo jacket, a silk blouse, pumps, or lace-up shoes.

Marie Courroy wears men's overalls by Lee with a basic T-shirt and bracelets from Autres Trésors.

Monday, Super-Skinny Jeans

The Iggy Pop style (skintight all over) is very demanding. It should never flatten the buttocks or prevent you from breathing, or reveal a tiny tummy. The length is all-important. It should spiral (or corkscrew) down to the shoes (think Jamie Hince) or extend to floor level, sixties style. Nothing in between.

Tuesday, Flared Jeans

As worn by Diane Keaton or Marianne Faithfull in the 1970s; or more recently, by Charlotte Gainsbourg posing for photos for Gerard Darel. Flared jeans lengthen the legs and emphasize the ass. If you're plump, choose them more "boot cut," meaning the flare starts around knee height. In any case, select a very long hem that virtually covers your entire shoe and opt for high heels; plus a fitted top or nipped-in shirt to avoid looking wide and one dimensional.

Wednesday, Boy's Jeans

The moment you find the right boyfriend, steal his jeans. If they're very loose on you, they're exactly what you require. While you're at it, pilfer a big belt along with the jeans and pull it tight around your waist. Tuck in your T-shirt or your button-down, roll up the jeans, and put on a pair of stilettos. No, you won't look like a sack of potatoes, even if you're overweight. On the contrary, boy's jeans can mask cellulite and folds of fat quite well. If your style permits, go for the tomboy look, with lace-up shoes.

Valérie d'Hauteville, Director of
Communications, dresses up her
Seven7 Jeans with a serious Andrew
GN jacket and two-tone ballet flats.

Sarah Eustis, an American ex-pat,
wears cropped jeans with Pierre
Hardy pumps and an Isabel Marant
blouse.

Priscilla de Laforcade in fabulous Isabel
Marant red jeans with Louboutin short
boots, a Heimstone bag, and a leather
jacket she found at the flea market.

Julie Bocquenet pairs her perfectly
distressed jeans with a white jacket by
Valentine Gauthier and wears lovely
eclectic jewelry that she bought during
her travels.

Thursday, White Jeans

Forget the image of white jeans and a sailor top. They deserve better than that. They're great in winter combined with a gray cashmere pullover, an ethnic tunic, moccasins, boots, or a trench coat. Nothing phases them. They can handle all our whims and all our styles. Not (too) stretch, they can be worn by women of all ages, and actually they can make you look younger.

Friday, Fantasy Jeans

Jeans don't have to be in primary colors or black. Vermillion, pale pink, Oshkosh-striped, waxed, studded, embroidered, zebra-striped, or with graffiti—it doesn't matter. We have a right to like them less conventional on condition that you leave the sequins, the spangled T-shirt, and the fringes in the drawer. Wear your fantasy jeans soberly, without extra adornment, unless you're auditioning for a show in Las Vegas.

Advice from Yaya, of Yaya Store in Paris, a Jeans Professional

"Jeans make you more beautiful. For example, if you want longer legs, they can do that better than anything else. The main thing is that you should like the way you look in a pair of jeans, even if they don't happen to be the ones that suit you best. Unfortunately, there's no universal advice one can give about them. Of course they shouldn't flatten your ass, make your thighs look heavy, or squeeze your calves too tight. The space between the back pockets is also very important. How far apart should they be? Again, it depends on your ass.

There's only one jeans design which more or less suits all shapes, and that's the 501 from the 1980s.

If you want to grow old with a pair of jeans, stay away from cheap ones. Their shape won't survive the test of time. Also, avoid "industrial" veining and artificial wear and torn effects in the wrong places, which are really tacky. Go out and buy a real, 100 percent cotton denim, non-stretch (on the inside you should clearly see a weft texture in sharp contrast to the outside). You should

Who says you have to wear heels with your boyfriend jeans?

never feel constrained wearing jeans, with the possible exception of skintight ones, which will loosen by one size over time anyway. But if your pair of jeans has never been washed, make absolutely sure you buy it two sizes too big for you."

Yaya's favorites:
Levi's Vintage, Edwin, Circle, and Denham

Saturday, Denim Shirt

By right, the denim shirt should be discussed in the chapter "As In Fashion, So In Life" (see page 50) because it makes our lives easier, with style. It's best worn in combination with something classical. In the winter, wear it buttoned up, tucked into a pencil skirt or a flared one, with tweed or Prince of Wales pattern men's pants, or with leather of some sort. In summer, it goes with a romantic dress or shorts.

Sunday, Denim Jacket

There's a clear rule here: Choose a jean jacket tight, or even too small. Treat it like a sexy, very feminine cardigan that you wear under another jacket or a coat. Don't hesitate to give it erotic intensity by wearing it skintight, with a lacy bra, a plastron necklace, and a loose chignon. The same goes for denim waistcoats.

· · · · · · · · ·

Five Big Mistakes:

- *Too many streaks*
- *Too many studs or sparkles*
- *Too long: Never turn the hem of the cuffs inside the lazy way— better to roll them up or make turnup cuffs. Otherwise, have them hemmed to look exactly like they did to begin with, only the right length.*
- *Too much fading: Wash jeans turned inside out at 86°F to prevent fading, with a little white wine vinegar in the water to fix the color. Also, avoid spin drying, which will break the cotton fibers.*
- *Super-narrow belts: Opt instead for a proper cowboy belt, or a belt that fills the belt loops.*

True jeans fetishists might like to know that there's a website that will repair their favorite pair for a few dollars: denimtherapy.com

Priscilla de Laforcade offsets her Balmain dress with a jean jacket and a Heimstone bag.

Interview

ODILE GILBERT
studio hairdresser

Is there such a thing as French style and if so how would you describe it?
Of course there is. As I see it, French style in fashion is totally akin to French *art de vivre*, to the French culture of good wine, good cooking, and a certain high quality of life. I really think that you cannot disassociate French fashion from this cultural heritage and education. I only realized how very French I was when I went to live abroad and saw how foreigners saw me. In the eyes of other nationalities, to be French is to be touched with a certain magic. Paris and France still symbolize chic, elegance, and refinement around the world. Fashion can take some of the credit for this, but it is also directly linked to our French national heritage. We share this education in beauty—and this love of a certain quality of life—with the Italians. It is no coincidence that all the haute couture fashion shows take place in Paris, and that all young fashion designers dream of one day creating their own haute couture collections. The elixir of couture runs unawares in the veins of French women.

What is your definition of a French woman?
She is self-sufficient. She immediately brings her personality to the forefront. Sometimes she dresses classically but there is always a twist to it. She takes less care of herself than her American counterpart. American women are impeccable, but I think the French strong point is the casual charm of their appearance.

American women are perhaps more glamorous in the Hollywood sense of the term. The French woman has genuine character, she can be conscious of her own attractiveness, and be interested in politics, cooking, and children as well. The fact that she likes fashion and beautiful clothes doesn't make her a frivolous person. They're part of her culture and her heritage. She depends more on charm than perfection, more on seduction than on an instant knockout effect. Simone de Beauvoir was a very beautiful woman, who wore beautiful clothes. Juliette Gréco was sublime and heavily engaged politically. The gorgeous, dumb blonde is an invention of Hollywood. In France, we had *Casque d'Or* (Simone Signoret), also sublime, also politically engaged. I think that outside France this dream image of French women still prevails—you only have to look at the success of the film *La Môme* around the world.

Who are your ideal French women?

I love Françoise Dorléac, who was beautiful but totally without vanity. She was lovely, funny, and casual. Her sensuality was more suggested than demonstrated. Modesty: now that's a very French trait. Arletty, whom Alaïa worships, was really the archetypal French woman, witty, elegant, extremely well-dressed. Inès de la Fressange, with her quick repartee and fabulous chic, is also quintessentially French. Sofia Coppola might have been French, too (but she isn't).

And this French chic, or French touch, do you think it still holds true?

I do. French designers are everywhere; they're opening more and more shops, in the United States and in Japan particularly.... Brands like Hermès have become major symbols of French chic. This is a brand with a real history and tradition of quality and savoir faire. When Victoria Beckham or Lady Gaga buy a Kelly bag from Hermès, they know very well that they're buying a piece of that history; they're obtaining not just a handbag but a symbol of elegance whose elegance can augment their own. In a way, they're buying themselves fashion respectability. American women consume vast quantities of clothes; we French are in the habit of keeping beautiful things— beautiful handbags, coats, and shoes.... We don't hesitate to bring out a fine Alaïa or Chanel piece from fifteen or twenty years ago because we know exactly what they represent.

What are the worst errors of taste one can make with hair?

Tints of three different colors: Avoid that like the plague. Poorly executed zebra highlights. Hair dyed purple— that's pretty awful, too. When you get older, choose the color that is a half tone lighter than your real color. It will lighten up your face. And finally, when you reach a certain age, white hair is quite lovely. White happens to be the one color the hair geniuses can't simulate—it breaks the hair.

What about hairstyles?

Your hairstyle is vital, as vital as the cut of your clothes. Avoid hard, strongly outlined styles. You need to preserve a certain softness and fluidity in your hair. It takes a hairdresser a very long time to learn how to cut hair well; it's a highly technical business. Yet all that technique must be camouflaged in order to achieve an effect of lightness. As one gets older, one should try to avoid struggling to look young. Instead, one should move serenely in the direction of elegance, sobriety, and chic.

THE BAG OF YOUR LIFE

YOU CAN EVEN BE UNFAITHFUL

It knows more about us than the love of our lives. We trust it with everything—sometimes with too many things. But just because it's an all-around receptacle, doesn't mean we should select it hastily. Modern marketing has made the handbag a must for all women.

Without necessarily yielding to the appeal—such as it is—of the "It" bag, we have to acknowledge that a handbag can make or break a look. Like your shoes, it has the power to impart lethal information about your style and attitude; a bag in cheap leather, a bad copy, or even a good copy will knock you right off the catwalk and into the crowd. To carry any of these is an error of taste that is all the less pardonable because originals are readily available, witty and totally uncloned, from young and gifted creators like Velvetine, TL-180, Campomaggi, MySuelly, Yvonne Yvonne, Tila March, laContrie, and Jamin Puech. And don't forget your mother's or aunt's vintage bag, whose leather is likely to be of better quality than anything you'll find today. It's well worthwhile to buy a really beautiful bag and take good care of it.

Antonine Peduzzi and Luisa Orsini, founders
of TL-180, carry their own bags.

The Importance of a Beautiful Bag

(and the collateral damage done by a nasty one)

• **It adds stylishness to your outfit, both when you're dressing casually and when you have to be more formal.**

Beware: Just like shoes, even to an untrained eye a badly made bag in cheap imitation leather with a botched finish and cheap gilding, or a shapeless carryall, will get you classified instantly as a person with no style at all. Maybe you can find pretty clothes for not very much money in the big stores, but there's no way you can do the same with leather bags. Nearly all the leather used to make mid-range leather goods today is poor quality—worse, if you buy it, you'll see bags exactly like your own on every street corner. One solution is to customize it yourself, using stencils. Another is to choose a highly colored piece made of fabric, beaded perhaps or ethnically inspired. As to the bag of the season, duplicated by the million and seen around the world on every bus and subway, it will only make you look boring. Can you imagine Sarah Jessica Parker, alias Carrie Bradshaw, carrying a gross copy? She'd rather go out carrying a little straw basket than be seen dead with Madame Tout-le-Monde's handbag. And if she had some money to spare, she'd spend it on something made by an up-and-coming designer—someone less known.

Claire Dhelens wears faded
Y3 jeans with vintage boots
by Yohji Yamamoto, a
camel-colored bodysuit,
a Véronique Leroy scarf,
and a beautiful classic
coat by Jay Arh and carries
the Claire Dhelens pour
Le Tanneur bag.

But the most beautiful bag won't go with everything. Bags carry more clout than you think, and they can wreck the way you look if you get them wrong. Hence the importance of owning at least three different kinds of bag, matching the different styles in your wardrobe, the seasons, and any special occasions that may crop up.

• **It ages well.**

Bags are not a question of name dropping—the quality has nothing to do with the label. Nor even sometimes with the price. The "It" bag, which costs an arm and a leg is not necessarily something that is guaranteed to last a lifetime. We have seen some of these bags' stitches come loose

after only two months. At the same time, certain specialist brands that may be less trendy know how to make bags of excellent quality and finish that we will never get tired of and that will last for years, even if we abandon them from time to time. So, take the time to choose your bag well!

● ● ● ● ● ● ● ● ●

The Difference Between an "It" Bag and a "Legend"

Not all "It" bags become "Legends." The legendary bag has lasted longer than a single season, which ephemeral star items seldom do. It has something special about it, something timeless, which allows it to go beyond the fashion of the moment. **Characteristics:** *It becomes more beautiful as it gets older (not something given to everyone), and it goes with practically everything (rare!).* **Examples of "Legends":** *The Kelly bag, which was created in 1935, is still not démodé, any more than its accomplice the Birkin, which was designed in 1984 by Jane herself. More recently, the Vanessa Bruno Cabas—one style of which is sold every half-hour all over the world—has appeared in different shapes and materials continuously since 1990. No doubt it is simplicity and pure lines that help these to prevail year after year.*

The real thing: a vintage crocodile bag.

Campomaggi bags are handmade in Tuscany from natural materials. The skins are weathered for a vintage look and the bags, like fine jeans, age beautifully.

. . . .
How to Keep Your Bag Fresh and Ready to Use

If you feel the need to set it aside for a while, vacuum clean the inside to get rid of dust, fur balls, bits of your children's leftover sandwiches, old candy wrappers, bus and cinema tickets.... If it's an especially valuable bag and you want to keep it in good condition, fill it with tissue paper so it won't lose its shape. You should have the same reflex when you go on a long trip: If you don't want to see it come out of your suitcase crushed like a deflated beach ball, stuff it with socks or a pullover. That way it will keep its shape. In your wardrobe, store it in the bag it came with when you bought it. If you've lost that, whatever you do, don't put it in a plastic bag, which will smother it and make the leather crack, whereas tissue paper or ordinary newspaper will allow it to breathe. When you get it out again, rub restorative moisturizing cream into the leather.

The ethnic-chic style of
the Yaya Store.

A fabulous yellow handbag by
MySuelly.

Inter
v
iew

MARION LALANNE &
PIERRE-ALEXIS HERMET
creators of IRM Design

Do you believe "the French touch" still means something?
Today's leading clothes manufacturers drown us so much in products that our eyes get jaded. All the same, we're not in any way obliged to swallow mass fashions. For us, French chic is embodied by a few of our friends who do very little to their hair, who don't even keep it squeaky clean all the time, but still remain elegant. The quality of being both disheveled and uncluttered is quintessentially French. Nevertheless, in France, women stay within certain limits. For example, even though we've taken the idea of torn stockings on board, in general we prefer to stay away from them. Nor do we advise anyone ever to show off their legs and their breasts at the same time. You don't do that. The strictly codified boundaries of French chic can be upsetting....

So you think that in France you can't dress exactly as you wish?
If I go out wearing clothes of many different colors, people in the street won't find it amusing, merely ridiculous. To avoid that kind of reaction we go into gray, black, white mode. It's quite true there are days when we're more sensitive and when we need to be quiet: In that case we know what kind of clothes to wear to go unnoticed, that's easy enough. But when I'm feeling strong I make myself up accordingly, and I'm not afraid to wear outrageous stuff. I do make the effort to create a sensation from time to time.

Who is your all-time favorite chic French woman?
I'm tempted to say Inès de la Fressange, but she's so commercialized and over-marketed that I don't think I will. Moreover, we're only twenty-two, and she belongs to another generation which came before ours. Charlotte Gainsbourg, with her androgynous figure, who isn't always beautiful and whose hair is sometimes a mess, is more inspiring to us. Diane Kruger, who is chic and natural, proves that women from abroad sometimes represent France even better than French women themselves.

Do your creations reflect contemporary trends?
In general we avoid that, but of course we can't prevent ourselves from absorbing what's going on around us. For example, during the sarouel [harem pants] fad it

was hard to imagine anything other than low-crotched pants. We also derive inspiration from generational trends: the simple pants-T-shirt-fitted-jacket look, which has been going on for years, still says something to us, and that's where our idea for a look based on jackets came from. For us, the jacket is the strongest item in anyone's wardrobe. Easy to find one in your size, it never goes out of fashion and it's a base on which to build many different outfits.

What's your pet hate?
I really don't have one. Everything depends on the way you interpret it. Even a dress with a low neckline front and back can be acceptable if you wear it with pants and a jacket. Pierre-Alexis thinks a woman should cover herself more after fifty. No more miniskirts and no more bikinis on the beach. Actually he hates anything mini....

Where did you get the idea for your glove bag?
Unlike a lot of other women, I can't stand the suitcase-type bag; I think it's ridiculous to lug a thing like that around all your life. Plus, if a bag is out of proportion it spoils the line of your clothes. I

prefer not to carry a bag at all. We developed ours after we realized that, and now it's the clutch bag of the moment. I take it everywhere with me; I find it very easy to manipulate.

What does "Made in France" mean to you?
It means French manufacture, period. But French manufacture is expensive and difficult. Factories are getting rarer and rarer here and they won't take small orders. Also, many

modern-day craftsmen and artisans are skittish with us; we're not very well known yet, so they don't always respond to our requests. It's very complicated. On the other hand, in China they really want to work, and they do it fast and cheap! We're trying to resist the temptation of using them. We'd rather have a clear conscience. Though we're still young, we owe it to ourselves to take a stand on this. To create in France, and to buy French products, is to be actively militant.

The cleverly designed clutch by IRM Design allows you to slip your hand inside to hold it securely.

THE LITTLE
BLACK DRESS

IS IT REALLY ESSENTIAL?

The little black dress is an ace in the hole for every wardrobe that takes itself seriously. It has the reputation of going with all shapes and sizes of women, of adapting to every situation, and of being timeless. For a long time it was the exclusive preserve of chambermaids, pensioners, and widows, before becoming the ultimate symbol of refinement in 1926, thanks to Coco Chanel.

All of today's magazines unite in prescribing it as a remedy for any wardrobe failure. That is true in theory, but in practice the use of the little black dress is rather more complex....

Michelle Boor wears a simple
dress by Aeschne and carries
her timeless Birkin bag!

Give It a Life

If you match it with the wrong thing, the little black dress, which is otherwise so refined, can quickly make you look like an inconsolable widow following a hearse, or a realist prewar singer (and not Edith Piaf). It has to be illuminated and made your own. Fine red lipstick and excellent stockings (anything but tights with holes) are the absolute minimum. Your bag and your shoes will position your dress in time and place: evening or daytime, chic or casual, conventional or wild.

Accessorize It

The same dress worn with bare legs and ballet flats will tell a completely different story when accompanied by high heels, tights, and multiple necklaces. Accessories in this case are not bit players: they are the stars. Black dramatizes and emphasizes, so be mindful of this when you choose your accessory—whether your aim is to be sober or playful, with real diamonds or costume jewelry.

•••••••••

Everything stands out and can be seen on the fabric of a black dress. Take care that not a stray hair, nor a speck of dust, nor the smallest stain spoils the beautiful image you dream of.

The statuesque Dauphine de Jerphanion wears Alexandre Vauthier.

Marilyn Feltz in a black vintage dress under a Véronique Leroy jacket. Leopard Louboutin pumps add a touch of color.

The classics: something
black and a "Burb"!

Actress Sonia Lezinska wearing
a Paule Ka dress and jacket, with
Sergio Rossi pumps.

Interview

ALEXANDRE VAUTHIER
couturier

© Photo Jean-Baptiste Mondino

The little black dress: myth or reality?

You could have a whole debate about the little black dress, but the fact is it's part of the established code of elegance. Along with white and gold, black represents Paris. Even if from time to time we get tired of it, we always go back to it, because it offers such obvious balance. Black is almost a uniform; it conceals things and only reveals that which should be visible. It protects you; it doesn't aggress the eye; it melts into the urban landscape and into the night. To wear a red dress is to convey an entirely different message: Red is the color of violence, passion, hell, love, sex, and blood; it signifies fire under the ice. It's the color that Spanish bullfighters wag at bulls to provoke them. Lipstick red has given the hue a more "couture" dimension; a woman in a red dress has a more sexual, carnal allure than she would if she were wearing black.

Do you think the French woman is still an example to others?

Even though fashion has become internationalized I like to think French women still represent elegance, chic, and good taste in the collective mind of the world. They have an ease, a lack of self-consciousness, and a classy urbanity that is unique. Chic New York women are more conventional. A French woman will always be more daring with her look and her clothes; she's unafraid to break with what is in fashion. It's no coincidence that Dior's New Look collection was so successful in America in 1950, because it offered a highly conventional image of womanhood in corsets and skirts.

In this modern world—which is so rapidly becoming homogenous—there is a strong desire to identify with that which characterizes and distinguishes French wit and allure. We possess a certain savoir faire and art of living that others lack. France is a country that has made perfumes, jewelry, foie gras, champagne, and wine for generations. We have a lot behind us; we have deep roots. The Avenue Montaigne, a street in Paris, is the absolute symbol of couture around the world. The French woman herself resembles Paris: She's chic, but she's also raffishly at ease in low company. She builds on this fine balance, she teases, she's elegant, she's humorous, she knows how to turn things on their heads unexpectedly. It's quite obvious why the little black dress convention originated in France: From a single piece of black fabric, French women fashioned an allure and a look and a timeless garment that can be worn by day or night. That dress has become the symbol of a certain modernity. It can be worn sophisticated, or it can be worn austere.

One has to be in tune with one's product. I think what I create has its roots firmly in France and I think the women who wear my clothes—Rihanna, Beyoncé, Alicia Keys, and the rest—come to me looking for that special French allure.

Should our clothes conceal or reveal?

Every woman dresses with a different aim. Some dress to seduce, others to make themselves look strong and capable. Our clothes always highlight and project a certain style. Dress is a language, almost a means of expression; and my clothes give women the means to express themselves. So they are revelatory. I don't believe that a woman should hide behind a designer, under any circumstances.

Do today's fashions inspire you in any way?

I think our era has lost its way. People have forgotten the fundamentals. Today, fashion is a business model and no more. Buying patterns and behavior have completely changed. For many fashion houses, what used to be plain luxury has become mass luxury. Clothes have become mere products to be marketed; yet marketing without a creative cell in the background is like a house without walls.

Is your manufacturing done in France?

Yes, because France is my history, and because there's still life left in luxury products made in France. If you buy them, you buy into an image, a history, and an identity. You can't wear a jacket that's been mass-produced to the tune of four million pieces in the same way as a jacket that is part of a limited edition.

Today, it's really boring—everything looks alike. The summers used to be short and blue and the winters long and brown, but today everything's possible and everyone's putting out the same thing, because everything's being marketed in the same way. Look at food—all those TV programs starring media chefs—that's the result of twenty years of steadily worsening cooking and produce. The same thing is happening in the fashion industry. In 1960, ready-to-wear appeared and smashed the model of luxury and couture. Now we've reached a saturation point and something new is bound to appear. The way is being constantly indicated to us by our commercial masters, because the consumer is so easily influenced; but women are only too aware that they're being manipulated and from this realization a new approach to consumption will emerge. We want more exclusive things, we want to rediscover ourselves, we don't want to be drowned in the mass. We're going through a period of transition. I don't know in which direction we're headed but there's no doubt something is happening.

What is your advice to women now?

Be inquisitive and demanding about the quality of the clothes and objects that you buy, because you're the one who will be living with them afterward. When you shop, be sure you know the difference between good work and bad. The same rules apply to the building of houses as to the building of clothes: Do you want rubbish that won't last, or do you want beautiful foundations that will stand the test of time? Do you want to arrive at a party wearing something extraordinary, so people will remember how you looked ten years later? If you do, you'd better opt for genuine quality, beginning now.

WELCOME TO THE WORLD OF THE BOURGEOISIE

HOW TO CLASS IT UP

The problem confronting the new bourgeoisie of today is how to respect classic codes without being starchy, boring, or dated. Historically, the BCBG (Bon Chic Bon Genre/Good Style Good Attitude) wardrobe, sometimes known as preppy in the United States, contains wonderful pieces that often cancel each other out when combined. It is their almost academic, uptight association that spoils part of the appeal. They have to be diverted from the straight and narrow, worn with the utmost awareness, and properly combined with items from other genres. Yes, bourgeois clothes can have special attractions. They can even be supersexy: It's no coincidence that the photographer Helmut Newton, the filmmaker Claude Chabrol, and the Paris winter collections of 2011–2012 dwelt on the erotic power generated by the codes of the bourgeoisie. However, when implementing this style yourself, there are a few do's and don'ts to keep in mind.

Valérie d'Hauteville opts for the simple and elegant look: white shirt and black pants.

Don't Wear

- **Gold-plated mother-of-pearl earrings (real or false).** These can be ravishing if they are vintage but certainly not if the mother-of-pearl and gold plate are fake. If they're worn in tandem with 1950s American middle class–type clothes they look fine. But the idea of family jewels, plus jeans, plus blow-dried hair should be firmly suppressed.

- **The velvet hair grip or scrunchy.** There's no excuse for this. It's awful, that's the way it is and there's no argument. This will not be mentioned again.

- **The slit tailored skirt.** If the hem is too high above the knee, people will focus on that part of the body, which is rarely attractive and often pudgy. It's no coincidence that Coco Chanel decreed that a woman should *never* show her knees. It shortens her silhouette. The hem should be kept just below the knee.

- **The three-quarter-length cargo pants with straps for tightening and pockets on the side.** These pants should be confined either to the hiking gear drawer, or to places where nobody cares whether you wear clothes that make you look fat. If you like clothes that make you look sporty with pockets, go for a real military pants or painter's pants that you can wear with sandals or ballet flats.

- **Pumps and ballet flats that cover the top of the foot.** With shoes of this type, if the foot is too covered, it gives the impression that the whole leg has been shortened, and this compresses the overall line. In addition, shoes that cover the whole foot often look like your grandmother's.

- **Broad pants cut too short.** Generally this type of pant was meant to be worn with flat shoes, which means you can't dress it up with high heels. However, without heels they usually look matronly. The only models that are flattering to wear with flat soles are tight ones or else pants that are at least tight at the bottom. If you really want to wear your bell-bottom pants stylishly with high heels, roll them up just above the ankles.

- **Pastel Capri pants and wide-cut Bermuda shorts.** These will ruin your reputation and your look. Is it really a priority for you to resemble Muriel Robin in *Les Visiteurs 2*?

- **Quilted jackets.** Tremendous in the autumn, when shooting in the Sologne region with a couple of black Labradors. And they keep you so warm! They are also fine at the Glastonbury Festival with muddy boots, fringed jeans, or hot pants and a handsome rock star's arm around your shoulders. But not otherwise.

A barrette by Hair DesignAccess adds an elegant touch to a casual ponytail.

Dauphine Jerphanion jazzes up an otherwise tame Isabel Marant jacket by piling on pieces of jewelry by Alexandre Vauthier, Rafia & Bossa, Marni, and Aurélie Bidermann.

- **Polo shirts.** This is the emblem of the preppy college style. Real preppies wore them tight with khaki pants (boys) and pleated skirts and blazers (girls). We would rather do without them altogether. The polo shirt's cousin, the polo dress, should be strictly reserved for the exclusive summer resort of Cap Ferret and the like.

- **Deck shoes in town with socks.** You can introduce them to your pastel shorts, lock them into a room together, and throw away the key. If you must have them, wear the real ones (Gucci, Tod's) without socks. Or just wear ordinary moccasins or espadrilles instead.

Of course if one has an unerring fashion instinct, one can succeed with these items. Kate Moss might even be capable of making us like the whole lot of them! Also, spare a thought for your hair: A ridiculous blow-dry will leave them no chance whatsoever. You'd be better off with the real dancer's chignon, or a ponytail, or a beautiful Jean Seberg short cut.

Dolce & Gabbana pumps with stone-encrusted heels.

Thumbs up for short
socks and Prada shoes
with a serious masculine
suit! And a man's watch
on the wrist.

Louboutin pump.

Wear

- **The V-neck cashmere cardigan or pullover.** Especially sexy when you wear it without a shirt underneath.
- **The pearl necklace.** You can wear this as much as you like in combination with a man's jacket (like Mademoiselle Chanel).
- **The navy blue blazer.** Also known as the Marlene Dietrich, wear it with a man's shirt and tie and perhaps even denim shorts. One can cinch it with a plain leather belt to add a rugged note.
- **The Barbour jacket.** You can't work it with short pants, but worn with a leather sheath and big boots it will give you a rock star/farmer look.

- **American moccasins.** Worn sockless with short chinos.
- **Ruffled silk shirts.** Worn with flared jeans, Diane Kruger style.
- **Liberty shirts.** Like Mick Jagger in the 1970s, with a colored sheath or tight stripy pants. Valérie Lemercier is an exponent of Liberty in all its forms.

· · · · · · · · · ·

The Muses

Jackie Kennedy, Betty Catroux, Françoise Sagan, Stéphane Audran, Françoise Fabian, Fanny Ardant, Inès de la Fressange, Valérie Lemercier, Vanessa Seward, and Anna Mouglalis.

Marie-Laure Mercadal, founder of Atelier Mercadal, in a Liberty shirt. She has several and always wears them with chinos or jeans.

Press agent Patricia Chélin in a stunning black coat by (No) Smoking Collection. Che Mihara maryjanes, a red leather Velvetine handbag, and a Sandrine de Montard necklace add a splash of color.

BEWARE!

Stockings That Make You Look Like a Grandma

Panty hose are unforgiving: If there's anything about them that is not pristine, they're disastrous. They have to look like they've just come out of the box. Flesh-colored, they have to be invisible. People should think your legs are completely bare; otherwise, the effect is altogether off. If you like them slightly shiny, think of Catherine Deneuve in *Belle de Jour* and there you have the only way these can possibly be worn, in other words, like in *Mad Men*, with pumps and a little 1960s dress. Nude panty hose combined with a straight dress cut just above the knee will make you look pretty vulgar, as they will if you wear them with jean shorts and boots. With a down jacket or Moon Boots, you're liable to be arrested by the fashion police. If you wear them with open-toe sandals, friends will cut you dead in the street. And if in spite of all this you still must wear them, at least try to choose a color that approximates your own skin and is above all not too shiny. As for sheer black panty hose, there are three cases for wearing them: 1) You're a nun, and you're wearing them with sandals, 2) You're Courtney Love's cousin and you've ripped them to shreds, 3) You're a school principal and you're due for retirement in a few month's time. We can only accept sheer black stockings on Dita Von Teese, whose femininity and sophistication is over the top.

Jewelry That Doesn't Cut Ice

Like a naked lightbulb in a hallway, there are things that one no longer notices, which one wears out of habit, but that other people see immediately. Medallions with names on them; souvenirs of children's birthdays, attached to little cords; Zodiac pendants; ugly rings; cheap plastic designer bracelets; clunky watches with clunky logos . . . Forget them. They can only do you harm.

• • • • • • • • •

All too often we pay too much attention to principal items, hair, and makeup, and overlook the tiny detail that may destroy the overall harmony.

Inter view

DAUPHINE DE JERPHANION
accessories stylist, Le Bon Marché, Paris

What is French style, in your eyes?
Personalities, first of all. And not necessarily indigenous French ones: I would mention Loulou de la Falaise, Betty Catroux, and more recently Olympia Le-Tan. Each one of these has—or had, in the case of Loulou, who died last year—the timeless quality that never goes out of fashion. And it is that quality that is peculiar to Paris. The muses of Saint-Germain-des-Prés, of the 1960s French cinema, of the Palace nightclub years, also continue to inspire us. Apart from fashion, there are stylish attitudes and gestures that are quintessentially French: Brigitte Bardot, chic and low-key, stepping out of a plane in a fur coat and ballet flats.... The voice of Françoise Dorléac, Anouk Aimée's corset in the film *Lola,* the sheer nerve of Jeanne Moreau, the energy of Juliette Gréco, the power of Grace Jones, the grace of Marisa Berenson.... These liberated, extremely feminine women are still the standard-bearers of French style. They will never go out of fashion.

Just like the "trench coat, Hermès Carré scarf, striped Breton Marinière top, and Repetto ballet flats" style?
Yes, because casual elegance interests us more than "bling-bling." We are keener on savoir faire than on trends. We grew up with the notion of quality and authentic couture. Well before the fashion for vintage clothes came in, French women liked wearing pretty outfits dug out of attics or passed down by their mothers and grandmothers.... We have a special gift for reinterpreting older fashions by combining them with new ones. That's one of the reasons why Isabel Marant works so well: We never stop wearing the clothes we started out with because they never go out of date. It's not the brand that makes you elegant but the piece of clothing itself and what you do with it.

Is elegance something that can be learned?
You have to start with yourself. Keep yourself clean and your skin properly cleansed. Make sure you have well-varnished fingernails at all times, and never wear too much makeup.... Learn to know yourself. If you try to plagiarize someone else, to copy a style or to be something you're not, you run a serious risk. You have to be sincere and have real conviction. You can make mistakes and be wrong from

time to time, that's nothing to worry about. You're bound to encounter a few bumps along the road to finding your own personality.

I wouldn't go so far as to say less is more, but if one isn't quite sure of oneself, there's no point in going overboard. For example, the clumsy manipulation of colors is very risky indeed. Like heels that are too high and shoes with ugly lines … and if you don't know how to walk properly, that's terrible, too. I need hardly mention hair with colors all jumbled up, tights in colors that don't match, soft, knit fabrics that are neither loose nor tight that go electrostatic on you and expose rolls of fat you'd rather hide, and short skirts associated with low necklines and high heels—very seldom attractive.

Hence the success of the little black dress!

Well, the little black dress at least helps you avoid catastrophe. It's a safety net, especially when you're feeling really down. If you've just been dumped over the phone, or if you're having problems at the office, the little black dress offers comfort. But watch out—there are Little Black Dresses, and little black dresses. You have to get the right one for your figure, not too clingy, nor too short, nor too low-cut. Above all, avoid making it into a uniform. And then do variations. Vary your pleasures! Never forget to accompany it and interpret it in different ways. If you don't care to look like a widow, you'll need to make yourself up right, fix your hair properly, and pick out pretty shoes and accessories. One day, you may wish to combine your black dress with colored tights. The next, with a Perfecto biker jacket. All in all there's no doubt that the LBD is a reliable standby that requires only a minimum of extra effort.

At what age would you say we need to begin exercising a degree of prudence in questions of fashion?

From the moment when you begin looking after yourself right and have found your own personal style, you can do just about anything you like. Of course, if you're any older than fifteen, you may wish to do without blue spangles on your eyelids, or legwarmers if you have broadish calves. All you need to do is avoid looking silly, know yourself thoroughly, and be honest with yourself.

What are the absolutely indispensable items for any woman's wardrobe?

Timeless pieces that you bring out regularly and regularly enjoy wearing:
– A pretty bag, not necessarily a fashionable one, with a certain comfort about it, not too heavy, with chains or straps that don't slip, well-designed …
– Flat-soled boots
– Pumps that are neither too high nor too flat-soled
– Silk scarf
– Large or small hoop earrings
– Trench coat
– Repetto ballet flats à la Brigitte Bardot
– Diane von Furstenberg wrap dress
Plus, as many accessories as you can get, because accessories have the chic to reinvigorate your wardrobe, remodernize it, and retell its story.… Without them, any wardrobe is so much the poorer.

STOLEN
CLOTHES

HOW MUCH CAN YOU STEAL?

Women have always enjoyed pillaging men's wardrobes. It used to be an act of rebellion. Today, it's normal behavior. Other people's wardrobes are no longer off-limits, at least not in quite the same way; you can burrow around everywhere, taking your pick of teenagers' clothes, professional clothes, sporting outfits, and military uniforms. The choice is immense.

Stealing from other people's wardrobes is another method of setting yourself apart: You need imagination to wear a piece of clothing from a totally different source. It has no references for you. You need to find a way of sublimating it. Here are a few places to look.

A man's hat from
New York Hat Co.

Your Grandmother's Closet

It's amazing how many treasures you will find in your mother's or grandmother's wardrobe. Vintage stuff, all of it within easy reach. Remember that before mass production really began, materials and finishes were very often of far better quality than they are today. If your grandmother is willing to lend, and her wardrobe interests you, you're sitting pretty.

Church's famous studded shoes.

Ruffled Shirts

The ruffled shirt, which recently came back into fashion, has loyal advocates who like to wear it décolleté or otherwise with jeans and a leather jacket, rather than in First Lady mode. They have embraced the attraction of this timeless garment.

Coats

Some of the patterns and cuts of coats designed between 1960 and 1970, with their three-quarter-length sleeves, pretty Bakelite buttons, and little round collars, are quite marvelous. Check carefully to make sure the size is right for you: Slanted shoulders or too much length can ruin the effect and make you appear outdated. It may be worth your while to find a good tailor to make alterations.

Handbags

We've all known lucky girls who've inherited beautifully made 1970s handbags or clutch bags from elegant, generous grandmothers. If you haven't been so fortunate, look closer; there is no reason to shun 1960s models made of crocodile skin or fine, patinated leather, or even genuine *skaï* clutch bags from the 1970s, which are always great.

Men's pants from Gap and Repetto dance shoes.

Scarves

Even if the secondhand stores are offering cheap scarves by the wagon load, never allow yourself to be led astray by any copy in polyester. Instead, make a beeline for the little square of silk, which will light up a working jacket, or for the long printed scarf that you can knot carelessly around your neck like a Bedouin.

• • • • • • • •

Other things we like: kitsch belts from the 1970s, Swinging London Liberty shirts, beautifully made pumps from the 1980s.

Your Boyfriend's Closet

Though you may wish you could, you don't necessarily have to be like Bianca Jagger and have your suits made-to-measure by the best Savile Row tailors. Provided the man in question is not built like a rugby player, go ahead and help yourself to his clothes—just about anything he has can be adapted for your use.

Waistcoats

The waistcoat is the third element of the three-piece suit. Marlene Dietrich wore it like a man, smoking a cigar. Diane Keaton revisited it in *Annie Hall*. In the last few years Kate Moss has raised it to the level of a rock star item. Properly tailored, with a checked or flower-print shirt and boy's pants; worn directly against naked, golden skin, in summer; with a romantic skirt; with a sheath and a T-shirt or a simple thin pullover … the waistcoat is an all-purpose garment. Steal it from your boyfriend. Or buy it for 5 euros in a secondhand store.

Denim Shorts

If you filch this article from a man, make sure it's in an extra-large size (unless you're very young and a bombshell, it'll be hard for you to carry off tight denim shorts).

Cindy Semhoun, an illustrator and the creator of the *Mlle Moun's* blog, balances her romantic skirt with a jacket from Zara's men's collection.

Boyfriend shorts suit just about everyone, even girls with generous dimensions. In winter, they look fine with thick woolen stockings, a tweed jacket, and lace-up shoes, high-heeled boots, or riding boots. In summer heat, they can be worn with an ethnic blouse or a man's shirt, *tropéziennes*, or moccasins. Can they be faded, fringed, or threadbare? Yes, if you're up to it. Yes, if you don't add anything else. Yes, if you're on the arm of the French singer Benjamin Biolay, not Enrique Iglesias.

V-Neck Pullovers

Like Rosemary McGrotha, the voluptuous *Elle* model of the 1980s, we like our V-neck long and loose with skinny jeans and pumps. Or worn with

leather leggings. It can also be belted if you combine it with a pencil skirt, for example. Or else you can try tucking it into a skirt.

Ties

We prefer the tie to be worn as a scarf, knotted twice above a shirt buttoned up to the collar and tucked in at the front. It can also be very pretty if you wear it as a belt, like Fred Astaire. Best to find it in secondhand stores or pick up your grandfather's backlog of ties; above all, avoid your brother-in-law's collection of Bart Simpson ties.

• • • • • • • • •

Also: white shirts, lumberjack shirts, jeans, pajamas, chinos, lace-up Oxfords and other heavy shoes. . . . You can steal them all.

Louise Hayat, a student, borrowed her grandmother's Chanel skirt and Dior bag and her little brother's school uniform jacket.

Jackets

A jacket can be too big on you, as long as it's not tent-size: We like it gypsy-style, unbuttoned, over a flowing cotton or silk muslin dress. If it's more carefully fitted, a jacket will give extra vim to an organza skirt or a pair of jeans. If you find that it makes your silhouette too bulky, cinch it at the waist with a simple leather cord or a boy's belt.

Use a tie to dress up a pair of classic black pants.

A bold combination starts with an Orla Kiely silk georgette skirt.

Your Teenage Niece's Closet

This is a trifle more difficult. There is a danger that you might end up looking like a wannabe adolescent. Use teenage clothes to add minor touches to other outfits—and above all, avoid wearing them in the same way that teenagers do. Otherwise, the effect is as pathetic as little girls in beauty contests who ape adults with daubed makeup and high-heeled shoes.

Creepers from London.

Hooded Sweatshirts

Never with jeans, but rather under a jacket or a trench coat. Wear it like a woman.

Denim Skirts

Absolutely not with stockings, pumps, or boots. And in summer only. With a tank top, a tunic, and flat sandals.

Patterned T-Shirts

Never with jeans with holes and studded boots. Instead, opt for an elegant jacket, fine leather, and ordinary denims. Certainly not pink with a silly motif (Mickey Mouse, Superman).

Claudine Collars

This type of collar was all the rage in the winter and spring of 2012. Will it make it through to the end of the year? Who knows. In any event, we prefer it in its most luxurious, sophisticated form, as promoted by certain top designers, rather than in the spirit of *Les Malheurs de Sophie*.

Doc Martens

Plenty of young—and not so young—women still love these British workmen's shoes, which were rescued from oblivion by the punks during the 1970s. We advise you not to combine them with an all-black look, but rather with something more feminine. The same fashion reasoning goes for wearing brothel creepers.

Funky Sneakers

These look good with leather treggings or a sheath, but grotesque with a pair of pants that are too sporty or stripy: There's a serious risk of looking like a millionaire soccer player just out of practice.

The Professional's Locker

When considering donning uniforms or clothing associated with a particular activity, like ballet or horseback riding, remember that, above all, nothing should be brand-new—only select used and patinated stuff. Customize them, dye them, wear them belted—but never wear these things as primary items.

Pants of Professional Uniforms

Painter's white, fisherman's blue, butcher's checks, and pump attendant's overalls—the latter were comprehensively photographed by Nicole Crassat in a series for *Elle* magazine in 1975. These things are all low-priced, long-lasting, and never go out of fashion. You can find them in shops that cater to professionals or on the Net for next to nothing. Worn loose, garish, stained, or immaculate, just as you like, these clothes go perfectly with heeled sandals or lace-up shoes.

Riding Clothes

Breeches, riding jackets, riding boots, ankle boots, gloves—just about everything from the riding world is good to wear. Except if it's brand-new.

White on white:
painter's pants.

Authentic army pants worn with a Chanel bustier and Sonia Rykiel boots.

Ballet Dancers' Outfits

Wrapover tops, tights that stop at the ankles, body stockings, ballet flats, tango dancers' pumps, leggings to wear around the house, tulle skirts with biker boots for going out: all these are more than fine.

Army Clothes

We're used to seeing reefer jackets, pea coats, and khaki military tunics everywhere. There are plenty of other military or quasi-military garments that can be revamped for our civilian purposes: overalls, aviator outfits, khaki shirts, army belts, and canvas ranger boots, for example. All these may be considered on condition that they're not worn as part of a fuller military paraphernalia, and that they honestly express your personality.

Stay away from soccer players' shiny shorts, rugby players' turtleneck shirts, and tennis shoes in town.... As to nurses' uniforms and chambermaids' aprons, they aren't appropriate for the street, but may be useful in other locales....

In the matter of wardrobe theft, anything goes. All you have to do is create contrasts. If you feel too dressed up, add a piece of sportswear. If the opposite is the case, put on a man's jacket.

Yaya FOUNDER OF THE
YAYA STORE,
RUE MONTMARTRE, PARIS

Inter*view*

SILVIA MOTTA
fashion editor of
***Grazia* magazine, Italy**

Do you think that French style—and French allure—are still alive and well?
Yes. Even though "the objects of feminine desire" today are much the same all over the world, I'd say that there's still one powerful brand of allure that can be found only in Paris. It consists in the natural elegance that seems to be part of French women's DNA. Fashion used to mean France. Paris was the symbol of elegance.

There is a sort of heritage, a transmission of style and femininity that sets French women apart. They've also been lucky enough to inherit a bible of fashion, published weekly, in the form of *Elle* magazine. *Elle* was the first modern publication to identify an original and different style and popularize it with charm, grace, elegance, and not a trace of vulgarity.

Elle offered women a new perspective on fashion: It showed us that you could be feminine wearing a man's shirt, and you could wear high heels with men's pants. It gave us the impetus to move outside the rules. Brigitte Bardot was one of the icons in this evolution of fashion and French society. Physically, too, French women had more modern shapes than others. They could be androgynous while remaining totally feminine. They were also carefree and wild, hardly made up at all, with charming faces, fine-featured, sweet and elegant, and they gave an impression of greater freedom. The Bardot style remains entirely contemporary.

Paris was for centuries the world's fashion capital. Do you think it still is?
I would say that Paris has been a trifle contaminated by Italian fashion (and vice versa). Hollywood, with its films and star system, did a great deal to popularize French haute couture style and American designers forced the ready-to-wear industry to change, by giving it a strong dose of street style. London is the citadel of unbridled imagination. Above all, fashion has gone international. There are fashion weeks being held all over the planet. Yet Paris remains the cradle of the greatest creative designers.

Perhaps French women are less inspiring nowadays than they used to be. Maybe that's because there's been such a total globalization and crossbreeding of fashion lately. You can buy the same identical dress in any city in the world and that makes it more difficult to pinpoint the authentic style of a French woman. A certain elegance is the only thing about it that is certain.

When I was traveling in China in the 1980s, I was surprised in Peking by the beauty of the women in their severe Mao jackets and the children in their traditional Chinese costume. The colors were marvelous and it all added up to a beauty, a grace, and a harmony that have been lost over the last twenty years. The Chinese today are all dressed like Europeans. I also love Indian ladies dressed in saris, and the originality and extravagance of certain young Japanese.

Do you think that fashion is inseparable from its time?
Yes, fashion really does reflect what's happening in society. Today, everything has succumbed to uniformity and

everyone seems to be wearing more or less the same things. Before the 1960s' economic boom, people went out to buy clothes only two or three times a year. They kept them carefully and they looked after them well. Today, we buy thousands of pieces of clothing without necessarily having anything in our wardrobes that suits us.

There is too much of everything, too much on offer. They have got it into our heads that luxury is something available to all of us, an idea which is the direct opposite of luxury. Women have been persuaded that if they possess luxury objects they will be happy. They've been made to believe that if they don't have such and such a bag or such and such a pair of shoes, they'll be miserable and wretched. Luxury has become trompe l'oeil. The universally available version of it is extraordinarily profitable and sometimes costs less to manufacture than it used to a few years ago. In the old days, local seamstresses copied the creations of the great French couturiers for their clients; today, the copy has become the master and it is that which has made fashion look out of touch. It has to change every six months, in a constant process of beginning all over again—and again. Each time it's back to square

one: Everything is some form of a remake, very few new things ever turn up. So now we have a genuine longing for new and different things.

What is your definition of a sexy woman?

To be sexy, a woman doesn't need to be in high heels, or to wear a dress with a spectacularly plunging neckline. Women who think that are rather pathetic. You see plenty of them in Italy, I'm afraid. But at the same time I rather admire a woman who makes an effort to be that extremely desirable and feminine—it's really hard work.

Italian advertising and TV have developed a feminine ideal that is sometimes way out of line. Before, the models were Grace Kelly and Audrey Hepburn; today, they're porn-star chambermaids. The references have become entirely vulgar. This vulgarization is also the fault of women's magazines, which have led women to believe it's OK to walk around town dressed in the same clothes they wear on the beach.

In short, we've lost the notion of respect for others, along with the notion of a dress code. It is simply not true that you can go to the office, *and* go out in the evening, wearing the same clothes.

Do you believe that our clothes are representative of our selves?

Yes, I do. We are what we wear. Our clothes represent something intimate and very personal about us. If we put on clothes that don't suit us, we make travesties of ourselves. We shouldn't make any mistake about what we want to project; the way we dress is important when we set out to gain acceptance from other people. I think the more-aware members of the younger generation are fed up with all this profusion of brands and images and labels, and they're reacting by dressing themselves in a highly conventional and conformist way. Whatever level of society they come from, the clothes they wear resemble each other very closely. They're looking for powerful symbols and they're trying to express their opposition to consumerism by choosing a neoconservative, officially recognized form of dress.

Your ideal wardrobe?

Overalls, a pair of men's khakis, a white shirt, or a pair of jeans, a classic coat. V-neck pullover, turtleneck sweater, tuxedo pants, high heels.

I also like dresses and beige combined with strong colors, and I often go out without my handbag.

SECONDHAND CLOTHES

HOW TO BUY AND WEAR THEM

Secondhand and vintage clothes are no longer the exclusive preserve of penniless students, now that many famous fashion muses have embraced them wholeheartedly. They offer an excellent way of creating a personal and unique look for any individual. They have nothing in common with mass-produced, soulless garments. The icing on the cake is that you can occasionally find secondhand clothes of great cachet and high-quality fabric and cut, of the kind which are rare today anywhere but in the most expensive couture collections.

Not everybody has the soul of a secondhand store buccaneer, nor is everyone eager to dive for rare pearls in piles of old tat. Indeed, some women are anxious about secondhand stores, see nothing in them, and invariably leave empty-handed. It is for women exactly like these that a whole series of stores has now emerged whose method is to judiciously select used garments in the light of passing trends, wash or clean them, and then present them for sale in attractive, tasteful surroundings. There are also stores that specialize in brand names and styles which are often expensive but just as often highly original and unusual. Venues like these are a long way from the rag-and-bone establishments of the back streets, and as a result they are liable to be pricey. However, in short, there is a secondhand clothes market for every style and every budget.

Michelle Boor updates a vintage fur cocktail jacket from London with a Chloé dress, Miu Miu socks, and Vouelle sandals. And of course, her ever-present Hermès bag.

The Bargain Hunter's Ten Commandments

I. Adopt vintage clothes gradually

If the already-worn effect turns you off, look for accessories that offer less evidence of previous ownership: things like belts, bags, clutch bags, and scarves. You're in no way obliged to take major items on board immediately, or for that matter to give priority to anything else on offer in the shop, notably shoes.

2. Stay loyal to your particular style

Go for the pieces with which you feel a natural affinity. Leave aside blouses with big flower patterns if you're not genuinely partial to such things; prefer romantic white blouses if they're what you really like.

3. Try something different

Give any piece of clothing with potential a chance to surprise you. A sudden penchant for a little green 1950s-style jacket can reap dividends, especially if you're the type who sticks firmly to black. Something like a handmade, crocheted top can spice up a pair of thin summer denims in a flash—and maybe the rest of your wardrobe, too.

4. Don't be a snob

Check for quality, not brand names. There's a difference between a cheap article you may wear for a joke one evening (a soft, sequinned 1980s blouse, perhaps), and a piece that's one of the pillars of your repertoire (a Courrèges coat, or a deep purple velvet jacket, for example). Thrift stores offer opportunities to find both kinds of clothing.

5. Pay special attention to basic materials

Steer clear of leather that smells musty (there's nothing you can ever do about that); avoid jackets with sweat marks in the lining, stained or water-damaged silk blouses, anything with holes in it or rust stains.... Read the labels, sniff the fabric, and check the lining. Make sure all the buttons are still in place, and that the zipper on a jacket or handbag functions properly. There's a difference between worthwhile vintage clothes and old tat. And watch out for fake aging: 1996 H&M or Naf Naf isn't vintage, it's just old.

Marie Peyronnel gives her Agnès B. jacket from the 1980s a modern look by wearing it with a Coralie de Seynes headband and black skinny pants.

6. Take the time to try things on

Don't pass on trying things on, just because they're not expensive. If you buy a piece of clothing, it has to suit you perfectly. Cuts have changed radically over the years: The fabric and style may be right for you, but if the sleeves are too broad or the shoulders too slanted or too tight, forget it. Unless you can afford to have it altered, that is, or can do the altering yourself.

7. Project yourself

Before you buy, confront the item with your basic clothes as you would do for some-thing brand-new. Does it complement at least one of your outfits, or does it risk becoming an orphan that will stay at the back of the closet forever? Will it add spice or a touch of color to a basic that you no longer wear? If so, buy it.

8. Don't neglect the basics

Never compromise on good workmanship when buying basics: the well-cut trench-coat, the perfect denim jacket, the biker boots, the thick woolen coat, the retro lace blouse…. This shouldn't prevent you from trying out a more avante-garde piece that you probably would never have bought new, when it was expensive.

Pauline d'Arfeuille, founder of FripesKetchup, mixes vintage—pants, Lanvin pumps, and a Balmain clutch—with new—leather jacket by Ventcouvert.

9. Vandalize old clothes for spare parts

It can be very worthwhile to buy a top just for its buttons, which may serve to add personality to a jacket bought in a big department store. A pretty fur collar taken from an otherwise old lady-ish jacket, or buttons filched from its cuffs, can breathe new life into an old piece that would otherwise remain hanging in your closet.

10. Combine vintage things with beautiful new ones

Above all, avoid the all-around vintage look. Once again—we cannot say it often enough—the secret lies in the combining. Combine your vintage, printed skirt with a fine cashmere pullover, wear your chicest pair of jeans with a bargain-basement lace blouse, or elegant boots with a vintage dress.... In fact, go for any mix that balances and adds flair.

Valentine Gauthier dyed her vintage dress a vibrant blue. A Valentine Gauthier wool cardigan keeps the chill away.

• • • • • • • • •

Do It Yourself

You don't have to be a skillful seamstress to transform a piece of clothing with your own hands. Sometimes all that is necessary is a pair of scissors applied to a university sweatshirt, to convert it into something much more feminine, with three-quarter-length sleeves and a nautical neckline. You can also change the laces of a pair of retro boots, dye a silk dress, sew sequins on a man's jacket, or add a broad belt to cinch a dress that is too loose. . . .

Interview

PATRICIA DELAHAIE
sociologist and life coach, author of *La sexualité est une longue conversation* (Marabout, Paris)

What can today's fashions tell us about our history?

The fashions have always followed the history of women and the evolution of the way they think. During the 1950s, practically all women subscribed to a certain model of femininity. They made themselves seemly and respectable, that is, they conformed; they were anxious about what people would say about them and seldom stepped out of line as individuals. In terms of clothes, this attitude translated into a kind of uniform. The majority of women wore dark skirts and white tops, with a few timidly colored variants. Family jewels were worn with pride on Sundays, demonstrating a strong attachment to family values and perhaps also to social success.

In the 1970s, during the hippie era, all the old chains were broken. After May 1968, it was forbidden to forbid. All constraints were sent packing, including dress ones: no more bras, no more belts, only long flowing stripy dresses and soft shoes.

Today, in the era of individualism, everyone can live and dress their own way, inventing themselves and the images that suit them best. Everything is possible now, including lots of fantasy— as is shown by the jewelry we wear. Your look reveals quantities of information about you; your clothes strip you metaphorically naked in the eyes of others. To what tribe do you belong? What image of yourself do you want to project? Do you wish to join the mass, or do you need to assert that you're different? Is it your intention to be seen, or would you prefer to stay in the background? Are you eager to express your creativity, do you need to display the sides of yourself that are sporty, asexual, or even rigid?

So dressing can be pretty complicated....

In any case, it's far less automatic than it used to be. It depends on how you feel from day to day. Sometimes it's sheer joy to dress; sometimes it's a misery (you've put on weight) or a real chore: you're depressed, you're down, and you dress any old way. What a shame!

Inter*view*

Picking out a combination that reflects how we are and highlights our best points is a marvelous way to begin the day. You may think as you dress of the pleasure you'll have when you see yourself in the elevator mirror, or in a shop window; and you'll look forward to the flattering looks you're bound to get from other people. Surely you must use this precious dressing time for yourself, give it all your attention, and turn it into a moment of genuine pleasure. It's the difference between gulping your morning coffee standing up, and enjoying a full, leisurely breakfast at the table.

Again, the pleasure of dressing can be experienced at one remove in the pleasure of buying clothes. Some women, I don't know why, seem to derive more delight from stuffing their closets than they do from actually wearing new clothes and shoes. For others the opposite is the case: The act of buying is a real struggle, but sorting through a personal collection and creating harmonious combinations within it are pleasures endlessly renewed. Often enough, a woman like this will buy a piece in a shop and walk out wearing it.

Are certain people predisposed to enjoy dressing more than others?
You mean, do they have a predisposition born of education? Yes, I think so. There are certain women who make you want to dress attractively like they do, because they know how to marry styles, shapes, and colors, and can see exactly what suits them. In certain families this is a gift passed down from mother to daughter, where days spent shopping together have bred a deep complicity. Other women, lacking that complicity, may need a model to help them, a sister perhaps or a friend who can transmit the taste for … well, exercising good taste on a daily basis. The most stimulating people are always the most creative, the ones who have genuine fun. Women like that treat dressing as a game. They invent something new every morning of their lives. They have something extra, like cooks who possess the art of inventing a delicious, original, beautifully presented dish with nothing but two or three condiments, a few leaves of salad, and a couple of tomatoes. Such people can weave infinite variety into a single theme; the pastas they serve never have the same taste from one day to the next. The same is true of clothes. There are women who know how to make infinitely varied use of the basic ones. They can appear to be dressed in a different way every single day of

the year; and like brilliant cooks making the best of their ingredients, they can enjoy the present to the full, observing with delight as the mornings, days, and seasons go by.

Is this something that can be learned?

A person's wardrobe reveals the truth about them, like the interior of their house. It tells their story. In a wardrobe you will see a blend of comfortable clothes, clothes which bring back memories, beloved handbags with the status of inherited furniture, treasured gifts, unwearable things bought on the spur of the moment....

Taking the time to clean out your wardrobe and remove anything that has ceased to have any relevance to who you are is the first step. After that, banish your prejudices. Do you need tons of money to dress according to your taste? No, you only need to like what you have—and maybe alter a few of your habits. As a rule, the parts of ourselves we like best are what we tend to clothe most attractively: the top if we're proud of our bosom, the bottom if we approve of our legs. We have plenty of manicures if we like our hands and fingers, we make up our eyes with great care if we think they're especially pretty—and we sometimes ignore the rest of ourselves. The trick is to observe and identify the bits we habitually neglect, because the greatest pleasures of dressing can be experienced only if we go about the business 100 percent. You can work this out for yourself, or you can resort to an image consultant to help you reach the same conclusion. Up to you.

Must we know ourselves well, to dress well?

That doesn't necessarily have to be a condition. But certainly if you're not sure of yourself, it's discouraging and you'll be liable to give up without a fight. Begin with the clothes you like wearing, that you feel good in: They will serve as a basis. Next, identify your psychological comfort zones. If you like tops, you should attend to them first. Bring in color, printed fabrics, and perhaps try a different style altogether. The rest should follow quite easily. Dressing ought to be a simple pleasure.

Some women think it's a futile one.

Maybe those women feel guilty about spending money and spending time on themselves. If you do that, instead of taking care of your wardrobe and making genuinely wise choices about what to do about it, you'll go strictly nowhere. You'll buy stuff too hastily and on impulse in the shops, or order it in quantity off the Internet. Either way, you'll end up with a wardrobe that's not only disappointing but also makes you feel guilty. A little like those ladies who oscillate between starving themselves and overeating, you'll swing between poorly thought-out purchases, and buying nothing at all. It's always better simply to enjoy the fun of picking out clothes for yourself, *and then wear them* … all of them.

CAN I STILL GET AWAY WITH THIS?

THE LIMITATIONS OF AGE

It's not our way to set limits and sell-by dates. Whatever your age, do exactly as you wish, provided the result is not a disguise and that it suits you. The aim of the game is to be one's self and not to copy models in magazines. Nevertheless, there are certain small errors that everyone should try to avoid.

Monica Goubin, founder
of the Monica brand,
gives her mother's fur
jacket a casual look with
a Monica skirt and top
and masculine San Marina
boots.

Adolescence, Camouflage, and Excess

Explore your style, copy other people, or go against the trend—there's nothing wrong with any of that. But there is something wrong when your makeup resembles a mortuary mask or the layers of Pocahontas ocher on your cheeks turns people's heads. The same goes for too much kohl on the eyes, the abuse of push-up bras, and the wearing of silly suspenders. They hate it when you tell them so, but teenage girls nearly always look more beautiful with a natural style, free of excessive adornment.

When You're Twenty, You Can Do As You Please

When you're twenty, you can party all night and wake up fresh as a daisy; you can lie in the sun for far too long; you can abuse alcohol and tobacco and eat chocolate bars at midnight without secondary effects, and your excesses will go unnoticed. Lucky? Perhaps not. The time of blessings can betray you. You may have to pay for it in full later, when you hit thirty-five, so you'd do well to counterbalance with a healthy way of life from the get go. Apart from that, as far as looks are concerned, life is wonderful. You can do as you please within the limits of your shape, your style, and your desires. It can be a time when you seriously doubt your own attractiveness and overplay your hand by piling on the so-called emblems of femininity: miniskirts, high heels, plunging necklines. But remember: Over-the-top is the opposite of sexy.

After Thirty, You Can Relax

In general, one has less time to look after oneself after thirty. One puts on a few pounds, one cancels appointments with the hairdresser, one forgets to update one's wardrobe and buys things for the children instead. It's not all that bad: If you've let yourself go a bit, it's also the moment to take yourself in hand and perhaps to find a style of your own at last. But beware of errors of taste that can make you look older than you are: streaky highlights in your hair, nails too long, cheap fabrics poorly cut, elastic blouses with straining buttons, an unflattering parka for going around the block, poor-quality denim, a cheap handbag into which you throw everything, regardless. Thirty is the age when you should be setting yourself apart by wearing really beautiful clothes—not the fashionable items of the moment, but the primaries and accessories that you really like and that reinforce your personality.

Ah, to be eighteen! Denim shorts and a blouse, a Mes Demoiselles bag, and Native-American-style boots purchased in the United States.

Shirley wears her own design jewelry with a Thierry Mugler jacket.

Forty Is a Time of Transition

You realize you're getting older in your body, but in your head you're the same as ever. You gain weight easily but lose it with great effort. Lack of sleep and anxiety can be read on your face and your whole outline changes (your waist thickens, your skin has ceased to glow with the same youthfulness, and your baby face is a thing of the past). Actresses say that this is the best age of all. We can believe them! Mission number one: Find a good colorist who uses a color that is not uniform but deep and lively. Mission number two: Take the greatest care of your skin with meticulous treatment and a properly planned system of makeup. Avoid the heavy makeup, lip liners, iridescent shades, and unsubtle color tones that age you (you are not in a Kabuki play). Mission number three: Always prefer the best materials. You can wear orange, red, and pink plaid trews if you like, but only on condition that they're beautifully made. Mission number four: Laugh. Laugh as much as you can! A smile is the most effective and beautiful makeup for the human face that was ever invented. And it isn't just actresses who say that. Our friends and lovers do, too.

Keep Laughing at Fifty, and Way Beyond

By now you know yourself pretty well and you can enjoy that fact. Even if your body continues to change, don't give up. On the contrary. Take care of yourself, apply the best moisturizing creams as regularly as possible, do yoga, and keep smiling. There's nothing to stop you from having fun with fashion, wearing violet tights and frilly lace or dressing like a boy, if you feel like it. Only don't bother anymore with "slut"-style miniskirts, worn with your back bare and sporting built-up rope-soled shoes. It's time to leave all that behind.

Be yourself: Dauphine wears her rock-glam style with ease.

66 Is there an age past that one has to stop wearing certain clothes? Certainly not! If one has the kind of style that goes with them, plenty of things continue to work. Doc Martens happen to be my thing. I love them and I photograph them all the time. I got hooked on them in London. To me the provocative, masculine, rebellious look of Doc Martens epitomizes freedom. I can run around in them all day and my legs never get tired. I give them a feminine touch by threading in velvet laces, or colored ones. I was congratulated by Doc Martens' London shop: They said it was so French, what I was doing. The thing is, we are all children at heart; it has nothing to do with trying to recover some kind of lost youth, only with staying in contact with the child hidden within us. So have as much fun as you can, and dare to be silly. Stay creative and unafraid to make mistakes. Yesterday, I went out wearing yellow tights, it wasn't a big success. Even so, I got compliments from a lot of guys! I encourage my clients to be daring: they're between thirty and sixty years old and are all fed up with the way the media puts them in the same basket with the same identity. They don't want to be stuffed into a mold. Here in the shop, I offer women a different approach to fashion. They come back and tell me that other people really like the way they look. Some of them don't even want to give the address of the shop to their friends—they keep it secret! 99

Catherine Lupis-Thomas
OWNER OF BOUTIQUE 1962

66 I'm not particularly bothered with fashion. I found my style very young when I was at school, with men's shirts, my hair in a chignon, and a pair of big glasses. I like classic things. My chignon for example: it's so anachronistic it looks off-key and slightly rock 'n' roll.... I get the feeling that there's really no such thing as fashion. In the street I see as many flared 1970s-style jeans as 501 Levi's, high-waisted '80s dresses or slim-fits from the year 2000. I see clogs, platform shoes, and kitten heels, too. There's no uniformity whatsoever. Every one of us has her own approach to fashion, and the more accessible brands like H&M or Zara offer a choice so wide that anyone can find something to her taste. Above all, we should not follow the fashion if it doesn't go with our figures. Fashion in the end is no more than what suits us. 99

Inès-Olympe Mercadal
ARTISTIC DIRECTOR, ATELIER
MERCADAL VINTAGE

All of these opinions were published in the blog *Mode Personnel(le)*.

OUR FAVORITE PLACES TO GO IN PARIS

CONCORDE
LOUVRE
RIVOLI

For Lunch or a Drink

Le Fumoir

Sink into a leather club chair; read the newspaper and talk about business, love, or clothes. Play the intellectual in the library, savor the charcuteries, indulge in the cakes.
6, RUE DE L'AMIRAL-DE-COLIGNY, 75001 PARIS. TEL: 011 33 1 42 92 00 24

Toraya

One of the oldest pastry shops in Japan has opened this refined and cozy tearoom two steps from the Place de la Concorde. Traditional cakes with poetic names, a dazzling list of teas; absolute bliss.
10, RUE SAINT-FLORENTIN, 75001 PARIS. TEL: 011 33 1 42 60 13 00

For Your Hair

Edge

This is where the top model agencies send girls to salvage their hair color—or even their hair. Using bio teas and natural pigments, they really take care of you.
10, RUE DU CHEVALIER-SAINT-GEORGES, 75001 PARIS.
TEL: 011 33 1 42 60 61 11

For Shopping

E. B. Meyrowitz

This charmingly old-fashioned shop has produced original and made-to-measure eyeglass frames since 1875. You can find the famous "Manhattan" model as well as a selection of their best frames since the 1950s. Fashionistas in the know come here to find glasses they won't see on anyone else.
5, RUE DE CASTIGLIONE, 75001 PARIS. TEL: 011 33 1 42 60 63 64

Fifi Chachnil

If you're looking for Hollywood movie star lingerie, this is the place. Fifi Chachnil adds her touch of charm and humor to bras, panties, merry widows, and baby doll nighties. Whether you're a fan of Bettie Page or Betty Grable, this is heaven.
68, RUE JEAN-JACQUES ROUSSEAU, 75001 PARIS.
TEL: 011 33 1 42 21 19 93

Frederic Malle

Malle, who is the grandson of the founder of Dior Parfums, has created a selection of perfumes with personality, allure, and character. He chooses the artisan parfumeurs he admires, and gives them a free hand to experiment: The results are daring, inventive, and delicious.
21, RUE DU MONT-THABOR, 75001 PARIS. TEL: 011 33 1 42 22 16 89

Gabrielle Geppert

The address for vintage Hermès bags. Also an impressive collection of Chanel, Saint Laurent, and Alaïa. If you're into fashion, take a lesson in style and quality from this passionate advocate of beautiful workmanship.
31, GALERIE MONTPENSIER, JARDIN DU PALAIS-ROYAL, 75001 PARIS. TEL: 011 33 1 42 61 53 53

Jamin Puech

Jamin Puech handbags are made by some of the best craftsmen in the world. Unique and timeless—not fashionable, but never out of fashion.
26, RUE CAMBON, 75001 PARIS.
TEL: 011 33 1 40 20 40 28

Librairie Galignani

This bookshop, which opened on the rue de Rivoli back in 1856, is one of the finest in Paris, with a wide selection of books in English, as well as many others impossible to find elsewhere. The atmosphere is unique.
224, RUE DE RIVOLI, 75001 PARIS.
TEL: 011 33 1 42 60 76 07

Maison Darré

Vincent Darré, who used to be a stylist for Karl Lagerfeld at Fendi, has opened this boutique of furniture and decoration in the manner of Cocteau's *La Belle et la Bête*. Very original objects.
32, RUE DU MONT-THABOR, 75001 PARIS. TEL: 011 33 1 42 60 27 97

Whitebird

You can easily lose yourself in this small and delicate jewel-box of a shop. The pieces of jewelry, from all over the world, are precious objects of desire. Keep this place in mind when you decide to buy yourself a well-deserved present.
38, RUE DE MONT-THABOR, 75001 PARIS. TEL: 011 33 1 58 62 25 86

For Dinner

Chez Ferdi

Excellent tapas, delicious hamburgers, good wines, a charming patron, and plenty of

top models. Always overflowing!
Reserve well in advance.
32, RUE DU MONT-THABOR, 75001
PARIS. TEL: 011 33 1 42 60 82 52

Le Restaurant du Palais Royal

Now in the hands of young chef
Eric Fontanini, this wonderful
restaurant looks out onto one
of the most beautiful gardens in
Paris. Eric is funny, bold, gifted,
and very friendly. He will (unobtru-
sively) stop by your table to chat
and you'll be enchanted by his
sense of humor and his passion
for cooking.
110, GALERIE DE VALOIS, 75001
PARIS. TEL: 011 33 1 40 20 00 27

LE MARAIS

For Shopping

Etat Libre d'Orange

With names like "True Blonde,"
"I'm a Man," "Putain des palaces,"
"Incense and Bubblegum," we're
in a world of humor and fantasy.
Started by Etienne de Swardt, Etat
Libre d'Orange is a declaration of
independence from the rest of the
perfume world. Bewitching, very
daring fragrances.
69, RUE DES ARCHIVES, 75003
PARIS. TEL: 011 33 1 42 78 30 09

Les Prairies de Paris

Is it a gallery or a clothing store?
Actually, it is both! Laetitia Ivanez,
the brand's designer, had dedicated the ground floor of her
second boutique to exhibitions,
while displaying her impeccably
cut, bright-colored clothing collection on the lower level. As for her
hats and ballet flats, once you

put them on, you will never take
them off!
23, RUE DEBELLEYME, 75003
PARIS. TEL: 011 33 1 48 04 91 16

Merci

In this enormous concept store
imagined as a gigantic holiday
house, one can lunch, have tea
or a drink, and/or shop. Here you
can wander among the creations
of Isabel Marant and Heimstone,
as well as those of lesser-known
designers. Part of the profits of
Merci go to charitable causes.
111, BOULEVARD BEAUMARCHAIS,
75003 PARIS. TEL: 011 33 1 42 77
00 33

Mes Demoiselles

Anita Radovanovic, an icon for
Japanese fashionistas, also has
unconditional devotees in her own
country. Frequently (but poorly)
copied, her filmy embroidered
blouses, featherlight dresses, and
bohemian sweaters are completely
irresistible.
45, RUE CHARLOT, 75003 PARIS.
TEL: 011 33 1 49 96 50 75

Minuit Moins 7

If you own a pair of shoes you
really love, here's where you bring
them when they're in trouble.
They're the "plastic surgeons" for
Louboutins and it's said they're
the only cordonniers who can
replace the famous red sole.
10, PASSAGE VÉRO-DODAT, 75001
PARIS. TEL: 011 33 1 42 21 15 47

Monsieur Paris

Gold, silver, diamonds … the
jewels designed by the subtle
Nadia are so light and delicate
you'll want to wear them two or

three at a time. You'll even forget
you have them on when you go to
bed —and that's the whole idea.
At Monsieur Paris they'll invite
you to watch the crafting of these
pieces in the workshop—not to
be missed.
53, RUE CHARLOT, 75003 PARIS.
TEL: 011 33 1 42 71 12 65

Valentine Gauthier

Valentine has no time for fashion
that copies and mimics. She
encourages her clients to dare,
and her clothes of mixed materials,
embroideries, leather patches, silk,
and metal rivets will make you feel
beautiful and different.
58, RUE CHARLOT, 75003 PARIS.
TEL: 011 33 1 48 87 68 40

Valerie Salacroux

Well known to all lovers of beautiful things—and for clogs that
can be worn summer or winter—
Valerie Salacroux also offers
splendid bags and totes in striking
colors. Magnificent raw materials
such as Basque taurillon leather,
along with fine belts, sandals,
and boots.
6, RUE DU PARC-ROYAL, 75003
PARIS. TEL: 011 33 1 46 28 79 09

For Lunch

Nanashi

This bio Japanese restaurant has
become a favorite for Paris' most
fashionable crowd. Which could
make one want to give it a wide
berth … only the freshness and
quality of the produce, and the
delicious bentos, are difficult to
resist. We vote overwhelmingly
in favor.

57, RUE CHARLOT, 75003 PARIS.
TEL: 011 33 1 44 61 45 49

Le Loir dans la théière

A foodie's paradise and the best lemon meringue tart in Paris! Expect to run into young designers or American celebrities stopping in—*incognito*—to sample French food. Be prepared for long lines, especially on Sundays.
3, RUE DES ROSIERS, 75004 PARIS.
TEL: 011 33 1 42 72 90 61

Marché des enfants rouges

Shop for the freshest food in Paris's oldest covered market—it was established in 1615. You'll find fish, organic vegetables, cheese, wine, and flowers. Come at lunchtime, sit at one of the indoor tables set up by the restaurants and grocers, and enjoy Moroccan treats, antipasti, or a bento box … everything is delicious!
39, RUE DE BRETAGNE, 75003 PARIS. TEL: 011 33 1 40 11 20 40

ÉTOILE PASSY TROCADÉRO

With so many *fast fashion* clothing shops lining the rue de Passy, it can be hard to find exactly what you want … but you can still find something special!

For Shopping

Franck et Fils

Typically French little/big department store. Recognized designers, an excellent selection of jewelry and accessories, as well as the creations of up-and-coming young designers. Cozier than Le Bon Marché or the enormous Galeries Lafayette; beloved by all.
80, RUE DE PASSY, 75016 PARIS.
TEL: 011 33 1 44 14 38 00

Komplex Store

Frequented principally for its jeans "bar," sourced from all over the world. You're bound to find the denim of your dreams. Also known for sober and masculine women's suits.
118, RUE DE LONGCHAMP, 75116 PARIS. TEL: 011 33 1 44 05 38 33

Le 66

This is the place to find clothes by the designers of the moment—and, better yet, those you won't find anywhere else. Over 200 designers are featured in the 13,000 square foot space dedicated to fashion and style. The latest fashion trends are presented in true "French style," not as they appear on the runway but the way only Parisian women can reinterpret them. This Paris destination is almost as famous as the Eiffel Tower!
66, AVENUE DES CHAMPS ELYSÉES, 75008 PARIS. TEL: 011 33 1 53 53 33 80

Maralex

Famous for its children's shoes, Maralex has shod every younger generation of the 16th arrondissement for the past sixty years. Today, it has modernized and expanded. Wonderful toys made of wood and recycled cardboard, books, decorative objects, as well as the never-out-of-style Startrites; also the creations of young designers like Louis Louise and Bellerose.

1, RUE DE LA POMPE, 75116 PARIS.
TEL: 011 33 1 42 88 92 90

Passy de Patrick Gérard

This shop is a treasure trove filled with brands like Mes Demoiselles, Campomaggi, My Pants, Star Mela, and Martinica Belts …
56, RUE DE PASSY, 75016 PARIS.
TEL: 011 33 1 42 24 02 04

Soeur

Finally, a brand devoted to adolescents. Domitille Brion and her sister Angélique have channeled their creativity into the strange age between ten and eighteen. They've hit on exactly the right language for girls who are no longer children but not quite adults. Here teenagers can begin to explore the Paris world of femininity and coquetry.
5, RUE PIERRE GUÉRIN, 75016 PARIS. TEL: 011 33 1 45 25 73 04

Swildens

This very attractive brand has expanded by exploring the fresh style of the 1970s, as well as the modernity of the new century. Its talented designer, Juliette, has been very successful in capturing the paradoxes and contradictions of today's young women.
9, RUE GUICHARD, 75016 PARIS.
TEL: 011 33 1 42 24 42 522

Victoire

This boutique, which opened a few years ago on the rue de Passy, is smaller than the original one on the Place des Victoires but the choice available is still top-notch.
16, RUE DE PASSY, 75116 PARIS.
TEL: 011 33 1 42 88 20 84

For Lunch

Akasaka

This wonderful Japanese restaurant in the 16th arrondissement has been around for more than twenty years serving delicious sushi in a warm and friendly atmosphere. Do try some of the authentic dishes that are always delicate and delicious. It's expensive but worth it.
9, RUE NICOLO, 75016 PARIS. TEL: 011 33 1 42 88 77 86

Carette

The 16th arrondissement's mythical tearoom. Early morning breakfast will be in the company of top businessmen and bankers; but around ten a.m., Carette becomes more feminine. By noon the terrace is packed with extremely red carpet thirty-year-olds.
4, PLACE DU TROCADÉRO, 75116 PARIS. TEL: 011 33 1 47 27 98 85

Comme des Poissons

One of the best sushi bars in Paris, but as it is the size of a pocket handkerchief, reservations are a must. Takeout is also an option.
24, RUE DE LA TOUR, 75116 PARIS. TEL: 011 33 1 45 20 70 37

Schwartz's Deli

This famous Marais burger joint recently opened a branch next to the Trocadéro. Authentic American decor, a long line at lunchtime, an extremely nice patron with magnetic blue eyes, and delicious hot dogs, cheeseburgers, and cheesecake.
7, AVENUE D'EYLAU, 75116 PARIS. TEL: 011 33 1 47 04 73 61

For Dinner

Le Paris 16

Italian cuisine, an inspired 1950s decor, everything homemade—and excellent! Plenty of atmosphere and conviviality in this little restaurant; habitués of all ages.
18, RUE DES BELLES-FEUILLES, 75116 PARIS. TEL: 011 33 1 47 04 56 33

SAINT-GERMAIN ODÉON

For Lunch or Dinner

Le Comptoir du Relais

Top-quality food for a reasonable price in a pleasant and sympathetic setting. A formula, halfway between brasserie and grande cuisine, which used to be sorely lacking in Paris. Yves Camdeborde, a béarnaise chef who has worked in all the top Paris restaurants, has succeeded here. We love to lunch or dine on the terrace, which is also open in winter, covered and heated.
9, CARREFOUR DE L'ODÉON, 75006 PARIS. TEL: 011 33 1 43 29 12 05

Les 2 Abeilles

Irresistible pastries in a lovely and feminine ambiance! A favorite of beautiful actresses, writers, and chic moms! Very Parisian and very delicious!
189, RUE DE L'UNIVERSITÉ, 75007 PARIS. TEL: 011 33 1 45 55 64 04

For Shopping

Eyepleasure

This shop is completely unlike most eyewear chain stores that try to sell you the latest brands. Here, the optician is a true stylist, who takes the time to get to know your personality and the image you want to project. And, you will not be wearing the same glasses as everyone else. The shop only carries eyewear by designers known for the perfection of their designs and materials.
40, RUE SAINT-SULPICE, PARIS 75006. TEL: 011 33 1 44 07 11 99

Heimstone

Alix Petit designs clothes for keeping, to be adopted and adapted by their owners. The Heimstone spirit is free and audacious.
23, RUE DU CHERCHE-MIDI, 75006 PARIS. TEL: 011 33 1 45 49 11 07

Ken Okada

In a dreamy cocoon of white tulle, Japanese designer Ken Okada presents her collection of cotton, silk, and nearly transparent shirts. Timeless but not exactly classic: several of them are reversible, front to back, and can be buttoned different ways. Four shirts for the price of one! So chic you'll want to forgo the jacket.
1 BIS, RUE DE LA CHAISE, 75007 PARIS. TEL: 011 33 1 42 55 18 81

Mona

The owner, Mona, chooses fantastic clothes that have seduced the most demanding clients (Diane Kruger is a regular). Pierre Hardy, Alaïa, Stella

McCartney ... here all is luxe et volupté.
17, RUE BONAPARTE, 75006 PARIS. TEL: 011 33 1 44 07 07 27

Parapluies Simon

Real umbrellas, parasols, and canes! Unique designs made by true craftsmen. No relation to the rubbish clandestinely offered for sale to tourists. This shop opened in 1897. They - and resew your old umbrellas and sell magnificent new ones—items not to be forgotten on the subway!
56, BOULEVARD SAINT-MICHEL, 75006 PARIS. TEL: 011 33 1 43 54 12 04

Polder

Two sisters who spent their childhood in Holland had the idea of dressing Parisian mothers and their daughters. We particularly like their tights and socks in acidulated colors mixed with Lurex. Ballet flats and very pretty handbags.
13, RUE DES QUATRE-VENTS, 75006 PARIS. TEL: 011 33 1 43 26 07 64

CHÂTELET
LES HALLES

For a Treat

BAM Bar à Manger

A dynamic neo-bistro with a creative menu of fresh ingredients, mixing various tastes: cream of pumpkin soup with ginger, lightly seared marinated tuna, glazed rump steak with garam masala, magret de canard with Espelette pepper ... Bar à Manger is refined and joyous.

13, RUE DES LAVANDIÈRES-SAINTE-OPPORTUNE, 75001 PARIS. TEL: 011 33 1 42 21 01 72

Blend Hamburger

This tiny restaurant serves the best hamburgers in Paris. The meat is produced in France and selected by Yves-Marie le Bourdonnec. Here, you can eat with your fingers. The sweet potato fries are not to be missed!
44, RUE D'ARGOUT, 75002 PARIS. TEL: 011 33 1 40 26 84 57

For Shopping

By Marie

A bohemian soul in love with beautiful clothes and delicate jewelry, Marie exhibits only what she enjoys and has discovered for herself: Forte Forte, Thakoon, Roseanna, Heimstone, Nessa by Vanessa Mimran.... Whether they're well known or on the way to becoming famous matters little; her aim is to delight and surprise us.
44, RUE ÉTIENNE-MARCEL, 75002 PARIS. TEL: 011 33 1 42 33 36 04

La Maison Momonì

Apart from the famous frilly panties from Italy, this establishment specializes in furniture unearthed at flea markets, deliciously romantic retro clothes and accessories, and little-known Italian lines.
36, RUE ÉTIENNE-MARCEL, 75002 PARIS. TEL: 011 33 1 53 40 81 48

Yaya Store

Casual cocoons inspired by 1960s American sportswear, the famous chèches in antique Hmong fabrics,

traditional dresses, bags worked in irresistible Italian leathers.... Many things you will find nowhere else are richly present in this treasure trove of a boutique.
55, RUE MONTMARTRE, 75002 PARIS. TEL: 011 33 1 40 39 92 89

MONTMARTRE
LES ABBESSES

For Shopping

Afwosh

Here you'll find many gift ideas (for yourself, your friends, your kids, and your sweetheart) in this concept store featuring decorative objects, designer jewelry, amusing accessories, and very reasonably priced clothing.
10, RUE D'HAUTEVILLE, 75010 PARIS. TEL: 011 33 9 52 91 44 80

Chiffon et Basile

An appealing selection of "casual rock designs": Laurence Doligé, Swildens, Scotch & Soda. Perfect for finding a great little sweater, boots, or a pants basic "with a twist." There are things for men as well.
86, RUE DES MARTYRS, 75018 PARIS. TEL: 011 33 1 46 06 54 36

Chinemachine

You're unlikely to leave this New York–style vintage dress shop without buying something. That is, if you can find your way through the mountains of 1980s-era blouses, flowered dresses, shoulder-padded jackets, and T-shirts for 5 euros.
100, RUE DES MARTYRS, 75018 PARIS. TEL: 011 33 1 80 50 27 66

Galerie 1962

Vintage furniture and lamps from the 1950s and 1960s, 1970s-inspired wallpaper, Orla Kiely radios, Marimekko dishes.... The owner of this gallery also has a nearby boutique, 1962, specializing in exciting ready-to-wear from little-known European brands.
4, RUE THOLOZÉ, 75018 PARIS. TEL: 011 33 1 42 54 28 08

Le Sept Cinq

Le Sept-Cinq is a mix of contemporary and vintage design. A modern-day Ali Baba might have selected the shop's clever and irresistible mix of offerings: fashions by young designers, books, jewelry, cupcakes, and handbags. There is even a cozy corner where you can have a drink with friends.
54, RUE NOTRE-DAME-DE-LORETTE, 75009 PARIS. TEL: 011 33 9 83 55 05 95

Séries Limitées

A pretty and feminine multi-brand shop that thoughtfully brings together the work of a selection of original creators, some of them private individuals. So Charlotte, Eple & Melk, Charlotte Sometime, Lucas du Tertre, Sessun, Virginie Castaway.... Impossible to leave this place empty-handed.
20, RUE HOUDON, 75018 PARIS. TEL: 011 33 1 42 55 40 85

Thanx God I'm a V.I.P.

Opened in 1994 by Sylvie Chateigner, this shop is full of sublime designer pieces (you'll find the very grandest here).
12, RUE DE LANCRY, 75010 PARIS. TEL: 011 33 1 42 03 02 09

Tombées du Camion

A fun shop full of pretty antique objects, old pearls, toys, brooches, belt buckles, and kitchen utensils.
17, RUE JOSEPH-DE-MAISTRE, 75018 PARIS. TEL: 011 33 1 77 15 05 02

For Dinner

Guilo Guilo

If you want to surprise an inveterate gastronome, here's where to bring him. A great Japanese chef very well-known in his own country; a single menu of eight dishes; around twenty diners at the counter slowly working their way through a succession of dishes, each more surprising than the last. Extremely refined and a treat for all the senses. Reserve a month ahead of time!
8, RUE GARREAU, 75018 PARIS. TEL: 011 33 1 42 54 23 92

BASTILLE

For shopping

La Botte Gardiane

Offering a French take on cowboy boots, this shop is known for its sandals and boots that are made in France and passed down through generations of mothers and daughters and fathers and sons. Quality and savoir-faire.
25, RUE DE CHARONNE, 75011 PARIS. TEL: 011 33 9 51 11 05 15

CANAL SAINT-MARTIN

For Shopping

Le Comptoir Général

This unusual and charming spot opens its doors on weekdays at 6:00pm. It is a bar, a vintage store, a club, a restaurant, and a thousand other things. The disarray and confusion only add to the excitement of this setting—a favorite of those who are attracted to quirky places.
80, QUAI DE JEMMAPES, 75010 PARIS. TEL: 011 33 1 44 88 24 46

Médecine douce

Don't be fooled by the name. Marie Montaud's line of jewelry, created in 2001, is exclusively made in France. Some pieces are actually made in the studio-shop that looks like a beehive and is located near the canal Saint-Martin.
10, RUE DE MARSEILLES, 75010 PARIS. TEL: 011 33 1 48 03 57 28

French-language edition design by Lucile Jouret

ABRAMS IMAGE EDITION

Translated from the French by Anthony Roberts

Editor: Laura Dozier
Designer: Shawn Dahl, dahlimama inc
Production Manager: Ankur Ghosh

Library of Congress Control Number: 2012033170
ISBN: 978-1-4197-0681-3

Printed and bound in Spain
10 9 8

Abrams books are available at special discounts when
purchased in quantity for premiums and promotions
as well as fundraising or educational use. Special
editions can also be created to specification. For
details, contact specialsales@abramsbooks.com or
the address below.

THE ART OF BOOKS SINCE 1949

115 West 18th Street
New York, NY 10011
www.abramsbooks.com